hOMEWORK'S * NOT * ANOTHER WORD FOR SOMETHING ELSE TO LOSE

Helping students WANT to succeed in school and then setting them up for success

by
Cheryl Miller Thurston
and
Bonnie Benham
Dawn DiPrince
Patricia Howard
Susan Malmstadt

Cottonwood Press, Inc.
Fort Collins, Colorado

Cottonwood Press, Inc.
305 West Magnolia, Suite 398
Fort Collins, Colorado 80521

ISBN 1-877673-25-0

Printed in the United States of America
Cover design by Patricia Howard

TABLE OF CONTENTS

INTRODUCTION

A number of years ago, one of my students cheated on an assignment. I was thrilled.

I was thrilled because he was finally showing some interest in school. Previously, he hadn't even bothered to show up most of the time, let alone turn in work or participate in class in any positive way. Cheating, in a backwards kind of way, seemed like a good sign. He was starting to care.

It's relatively easy to reach students who care. Unfortunately, schools today have too many students who seem alienated from everything about school, students who seem to float through the system, uncaring and unconnected. They often have no thought of a future beyond next week or next summer. Even the good students sometimes have little understanding of many of the important benefits of an education.

Many schools find little success with traditional approaches to teaching what are loosely defined as "study skills." Lessons on how to use a weekly organizer are pretty useless to a student who loses his organizer on the way to lunch and doesn't even notice it is missing. Lessons on how to take notes are pointless for a student who doesn't bring paper and pencil to class. Tips on taking essay tests are not very helpful to someone who hasn't seen her textbook in six or seven weeks and who has been absent three days a week all semester.

Most approaches to helping students succeed in school are missing a crucial step — helping them WANT to succeed. Before we can teach how to succeed, we have to convince some students that succeeding in school is a worthwhile endeavor at all.

And that's why my four colleagues and I have written this book. We believe that students need to understand the importance of education in a down-to-earth way that makes sense to them. We want to entice them to look at the future, to think about what they want in life. We want to encourage them to set goals, to look forward in a positive way and to see how education can help broaden their horizons. *Then* we want to help set them up for success by addressing such subjects as attitude and habits.

We have tried to write a book that is honest in its approach to school success. For example, we do not tell students, as so many books do, that they should study at a desk in a quiet place, with a good lamp. The truth is that good students all over the United States thrive by studying while sprawled out on their beds, with music in the background and a bag of potato chips nearby. The truth is that *some* students work best at a quiet desk, but others do not. Students need to figure out what works best for them — not what they *like* best, but what really *works* best. People are different, and there are many "right" approaches to learning.

One final note: We believe that life success is more important than school success. The point of learning is not "to do well in college." Education is valuable to *all* students, college-bound or not. *Homework's Not Another Word for Something Else to Lose* is designed to appeal to a wide variety of students, from at-risk to gifted-and-talented. We hope that it will help *your* students set themselves up for success.

Cheryl Miller Thurston

Helping Students ☆ WANT ☆ to Succeed

Helping Students WANT to Succeed

The activities in this chapter are designed to help students see the importance of education.

For some students, that may be a stretch. These are the students who have stopped caring about school at all, or who never cared in the first place — or the ones who have learned to cover up their failures with an attitude that says, "So what?" The activities will help these students see, or start to see, that school success is a goal worth pursuing.

For students who already recognize the importance of education, the activities will strengthen their commitment and help them look at knowledge in new ways. Some may begin to understand the importance of thinking about the future. Others may get beyond "good grades" and look towards a higher goal — learning.

For maximum benefit, use the activities in sequence, especially if you are teaching an entire unit or class on study skills. Or feel free to pick and choose among the activities to supplement your regular classroom lessons. While the activities may not fit the specific curriculum goals for your subject area, they will help create *attitudes* that will make reaching those goals much easier, for both you and your students.

Teacher Instructions
for
Knowledge — Why?

The point of "Knowledge — Why?" is to help students think about why education is important, without preaching to them. The activity includes six reasons why knowledge is important, with real-life examples to back them up. Read aloud the examples with your students and discuss them. Then have them come up with two more examples to illustrate each reason. Many students will be able to contribute examples from the lives of family or friends. If they can't, encourage them to imagine scenarios that *might* reasonably occur.

It is often helpful to stretch this activity out over several days, allowing time for students to think about each reason and perhaps even ask their families for help in coming up with examples. You might also ask students to discuss or write about the quotations that precede each reason. What do they think the quotations mean? Do the quotations apply to their own lives?

Knowledge — Why?

Not to know is bad. Not to want to know is worse.

—West African proverb

A school day can be filled to overflowing with lessons, friends, homework, sports and other activities. It is easy to lose sight of why we even go to school.

The reason, of course, is to learn, to gain knowledge. But why do we need knowledge?

Knowledge is sometimes hard to define. No one can touch, see, hear, taste or smell it. Because it is hard to "grab hold of," it is sometimes hard to understand why knowledge is important.

It *is* important, though — very important. On the following pages are seven reasons why knowledge is important in today's world. See if you can add to the examples listed after each reason. Your examples can be from real life, or they can be examples that you can imagine *might* reasonably happen.

A discovery is said to be an accident meeting a prepared mind.
— Albert Szent-Gyorgyi

Knowledge is power

According to some people, two things make a person powerful in our world today — money and knowledge. Money can be hard to get. Knowledge, however, is available to nearly anyone.

How can knowledge make a person powerful? Here are just a few examples:

- Damion is a highly skilled computer programmer. He has the power to create software that can change people's lives, making their businesses run more efficiently and giving them more time to spend with their families. Because he is so knowledgeable, many firms want to hire him. His knowledge brings him a high salary because the company he works for now must pay him well in order to keep him from going somewhere else.

- Nicole's knowledge of writing helps her in numerous ways. She is very convincing. When she writes a letter of complaint to the president of a company, her letter gets results. When she sends a letter to the editor to the newspaper, she changes people's minds. The local library changed the way it handles fines; a university changed the way it handles job interviews; and a car dealership changed the way it treats customers — all because of Nicole's powerful letters.

- Brett is not a specialist at anything. He does, however, have a lot of knowledge about how the library works. Whenever he needs to know anything, from how to pick a good VCR to how to choose garden plants that will grow well where he lives, he goes to the library. He has the power to find out just about anything he wants to know in life.

Think of at least two more examples of how knowledge can give a person power:

(1) _____

   _____

   _____

   _____

(2) _____

   _____

   _____

   _____

Every fact that is learned becomes a key to other facts.

— E.L. Youmans

Knowledge gives you choices

With knowledge, you have many more choices available to you in life. For example, if you know basic math skills, you can choose a job that requires basic math skills. That doesn't mean that you *have to* choose a job that requires basic math skills. It means that you have a choice. If you can't do basic math, you rule yourself out of the hundreds of jobs in the world that require basic math skills.

Here are three more examples of how knowledge gives you choices and options:

- Mary took a course in auto mechanics in high school. Now, when she is low on money, she has a choice not available to many of her friends: She can do simple repairs and maintenance herself, instead of taking her car to a garage.

- Su Li graduated from high school. Many jobs are open to her that are not open to her brother Tan, who dropped out in tenth grade. Su Li has more choices than Tan.

- Cody always thought he wanted to be a musician when he grew up. He tried to make it in a band, but he found that the competition was just too tough. He decided to go back to school and become a landscape architect. Fortunately, he had a lot of knowledge of plants and a strong background in art. His knowledge gave him the options he wouldn't have had otherwise, and he was accepted into the landscape architecture program.

Think of two more examples of how knowledge can give a person choices and options.

(1) _____

_____

_____

_____

(2) _____

_____

_____

_____

The Brain is wider than the Sky —

— Emily Dickinson

Knowledge opens up the world

What if a person grew up in one small town, never seeing books, never seeing television, never having contact with anyone outside of that town? Obviously, that person would have a very narrow view of the world. He or she would have no way to imagine what life *could* be like and *is* like in other places.

Knowledge opens up the world to people by helping them to learn about things they might never experience on their own. Here are three examples:

- Jerry is a serious artist, and he would love to travel to Paris and visit the Louvre, the national museum where many famous works of art are on display. However, his family doesn't have the money to send him. Jerry decided to read everything he could about the Louvre and about the artists and their works. His world was expanded, though he never physically left his hometown, and he feels that his painting has improved as well.

- Elizabeth never thought much about prejudice, since she lives in a town where there are very few minorities. Then she read some autobiographies about famous writers, athletes, musicians and American leaders from various minority groups. She saw how prejudice hurt them and held them back, and her eyes were opened. She now has a greater understanding of the difficulties minority groups have faced in this country's history.

- Alex Benham never even heard of "genealogy" until he stumbled upon a book about it in his grandmother's study. Now he is seeing his family in a whole new way as he researches his family tree and learns about how and why his ancestors came to this country. "I'm proud to be a Benham now," he explains.

Think of two more examples of ways that knowledge can open up the world to a person:

(1) _____

_____

_____

_____

(2) _____

_____

_____

_____

Somewhere, something incredible is waiting to be known.

— Carl Sagan

Knowledge makes you independent

One of the best things about knowledge is that it makes you more independent. You can make more intelligent decisions when *you* are in charge of your life.

Here are three examples of how knowledge can make you independent:

- Calvin, 25, used to lose a lot of money because of charges from his bank for "insufficient funds." He didn't know how to balance his checkbook and didn't know when he was overdrawn. He felt nervous every time he wrote a check. When he had to borrow money from his parents, he felt like a child.

    Finally, he got help and learned how to manage his finances. Now he feels good about taking care of himself, and he feels that his parents respect him more, too.

- Rosa recently had to move to a new town to help care for her aging parents. She knows a lot about selling houses, and she is good at it. Her knowledge helped her get a job quickly, and she didn't have to worry about how she was going to support herself and her two small children.

- Antonio's grandmother came to America as a young woman and never learned to drive a car. She lived on a farm with no access to public transportation. Whenever she needed something at the store, she had to call a relative or friend for a ride, or she had to get her husband to take her. She could never go to a movie, meet a friend for lunch or go to Antonio's soccer games, unless someone else could provide transportation.

    Then her husband had a heart attack and died. At a time when she was struggling with grief and depression, she also had to struggle with the helpless feeling of not being able to get around on her own.

    Finally, at age 63, Antonio's grandmother learned to drive. She felt as though a huge weight had been lifted from her shoulders. "I feel free!" she told Antonio proudly. "I can go wherever I want, whenever I want, without depending others."

Think of two more examples of ways that knowledge might make you independent:

(1) _____

_____

_____

_____

(2) _____

_____

_____

_____

The human mind, once stretched to a new idea, never goes back to its original dimensions.
— Oliver Wendell Holmes

Knowledge makes you interesting

People without knowledge can be pretty boring. What do they have to talk about? What do they have to contribute to a conversation?

Knowledge adds spice to our personalities. That doesn't mean that we have to go around lecturing people with our knowledge. It just means that we can hold up our end of a conversation.

Here are three examples of knowledge making a person interesting:

- Jenna has traveled all over the world with her family. She has fascinating stories about different customs all over the world, and people love to listen to her.

- Brad knows just about everything there is to know about comic books, from their history to which ones are most valuable today. When he talks about comics, his face lights up, and even people who aren't interested in comics find it interesting to hear about what *he* finds so interesting.

- Crystal knows a little bit about just about everything, from sports trivia and skiing to politics and American history. Her knowledge helps her ask intelligent questions and get others talking about all kinds of subjects. Her interest in them makes *her* seem interesting.

Now think of two more examples of how knowledge can make a person interesting:

(1) _____

_____

_____

_____

(2) _____

_____

_____

_____

He who has imagination without learning has wings but no feet.

— Joubert

Knowledge is the ticket to newer and better ways of life

If you ever want to change your life or to improve it, knowledge is often the key.

Perhaps you like your life just fine the way it is. That's great. But what if your life changes? What if your circumstances change? What if changes happen that are beyond your control?

Some changes happen *to* us. Knowledge can help us make the best of those changes. Other changes happen because we *make* them happen. Knowledge is the key to making them happen.

Here are three examples of how knowledge can lead to life changes:

• Jesse lived with his wife and children in a small town in Florida. A hurricane two years ago wiped out his home and his small dry cleaning business. Jesse had change forced upon him. He had to deal with it.
What did he do? He decided to start over in another area of the country in a new business. He read everything he could about fast food franchises and sources of money for new businesses. His wife researched areas of the country where they would like to live. Their knowledge led them, eventually, to a new life in Arizona. So far, they are very pleased with the change.

• After only a month, Meredith got sick of working as a maid in a motel. However, she couldn't find any other work in her town because she hadn't graduated from high school. Like many dropouts, she was intelligent. She studied for the General Educational Development (GED) test and passed. Then she saved her money and enrolled in a writing course at a local community college. She discovered that she loved to write and had a talent for it. She learned everything she could about writing, while continuing to work as a motel maid. It took her a long time, but she was eventually able to earn a scholarship to go back to school full-time. Today Meredith is working as a copy writer at an ad agency, and at night she is writing a novel for young adults.

• Casey loved hiking, skiing, swimming, camping — anything he could do out-of-doors. He worked in a series of fast food jobs, just to earn enough to get by. Then he spent his weekends camping and hiking.
Finally, Casey decided he wanted more. He wanted to be his own boss. He wanted to earn enough money so that he wasn't constantly struggling. He bought a book on careers and took some aptitude tests. His solution? He decided that he would like to run a rafting business, directing rafting trips in the Rocky Mountains.
Casey saw right away that he needed some basic knowledge about running a business, so he signed up for a basic accounting course. He also started reading everything he could about starting a business. He realized that knowledge can come from people as well as books. He interviewed people who had started their own businesses, and he

interviewed travel agents who book tours for people. "What are you looking for?" he asked. "What are your clients looking for?"

It took him two years, but Casey finally felt he had the knowledge he needed to start his business. With the financial backing of a partner, he started a business called "Outdoor Adventures." He now leads camping, hiking, rafting and skiing tours for tourists from all over the country. The business is new, so he still doesn't have much money. However, he spends nearly every day doing what he loves — rafting, hiking, camping and skiing.

Think of two more examples of how knowledge can lead to a newer and better way of life.

(1) _____

_____

_____

_____

(2) _____

_____

_____

_____

Can you think of any more reasons why knowledge is important? List your reasons below.

_____

_____

_____

_____

_____

_____

_____

_____

_____

_____

Teacher Instructions for

Reality Check ✓

"Reality Check" helps students take a serious look at the expenses they are likely to have as an adult. In helping your students complete the activity, remember that the point is for them to determine whether or not their expectations about the future are realistic. It isn't necessary that every single detail be absolutely accurate. It *is* necessary that they take a realistic look at the expenses a responsible adult is likely to face.

Many young people are surprised, for example, that a job as a receptionist is unlikely to support a single mom and two preschoolers living in a three-bedroom home in the suburbs, at least not all by itself. They are disturbed to learn that costs like rent and health insurance take a severe bite out of the money they had hoped to spend on traveling around the world or buying a Porsche.

This activity is designed as a look at the future for *responsible, law-abiding adults.* Therefore, a few more ground rules apply:

- An individual's income cannot come from something illegal, like drug dealing, counterfeiting, smuggling, etc.
- Bankruptcy is not an option.
- Income cannot come from government subsidies.
- Individuals must be living on their own. (Planning to move back in with their parents to save money is not an option.)
- Individuals cannot break the law. (If automobile insurance is required in your state, they cannot choose to save money by not paying for automobile insurance.)

Encourage students to use their parents and other adults for help in completing this exercise. Parents are usually very supportive and eager to help their children see that money does not, indeed, grow on trees. They may even be willing to send in copies of actual bills to help students collect information.

Determining income

Before students look at their expenses, they will need to determine their approximate income. Have students select a career that they think might at least be a good possibility for them. (Some students may even want to complete the activity more than once, using different careers as a basis for their income.)

Encourage students to consider a wide-range of occupations, but remind them to be realistic. Someone who hates science and math probably shouldn't be planning to become a nuclear physicist. Someone who wants to travel all over the world in luxury probably shouldn't plan on a career as a convenience store clerk.

In determining income, have students use an average salary or wage for a person who has been working in a position for five years or less. They can use any of a number of sources to determine that figure: classified ads, the library, the school counselor, personnel offices, professionals in the field, parents and people they know in the field.

Determining expenses

In helping students list their expenses, it is easiest to have them base their figures on today's prices in your area of the country. (However, if you live in a rural area out west and a student plans to live in downtown Manhattan, you might want to have that student do some research about prices in New York City.)

Remind students that they are coming up with *approximate* costs, based on today's prices. The idea is to help them look at the future more realistically, not to pin them down to certainty. For some groups, bringing in play money can be helpful. Students can more easily visualize how much money they have and where it needs to go.

Before you get started

Before you give the activity to your students, it is helpful to do a demonstration with the class. Pick a career ahead of time, and ask a student to come forward and "be" an adult with that career.

First give the student his or her monthly wages, in play money. Immediately after that, take back the amount someone at that wage level is likely to pay for taxes.

Then become the bill collector. Go down the list of expenses listed on pages 23-26 and have the student pay what you have determined ahead of time to be reasonable amounts for each item.

Clarify any items that seem confusing to students, and discuss solutions to any problems that an individual might have making ends meet. Then have students complete the exercise for themselves.

Discussion

After students have completed the activity, ask them to discuss or write about their observations. What surprised them? What did not? What did they learn?

This exercise can be a real eye opener for most students, as well as one of the most helpful exercises they will ever complete in school.

Reality Check ✓

Why is there so much month left at the end of the money?

— Unknown

There are no instruction books for being an adult. People have to discover a lot on their own, sometimes the hard way.

Try your own reality check about adulthood. Choose an age when you think you will have been out of school for at least five years. (That age might be 20 for one person and 32 for someone else.) Choose a job that *you* think is a good possibility for you.

Now do a budget for yourself, using the questions below to help you plan. When the questions concern money, base your answers on today's prices. Use newspaper ads, adults you know and any other reasonable sources to help you find information. You might also want to have a calculator handy.

Me, at age _____

Of course you can't be sure what you will be doing in the future. Choose what you think are *likely* possibilities in answering the questions about your possible future life:

Income

What is your job? _____

How much are you earning, per month?   1. $ _____

How much of your income is withheld for income tax? 2. $ _____

What is your total available income?   3. $ _____
Available income is what you have to work with after taxes.
To get this figure, subtract the amount in the gray box (#2) from
the amount in the top white box (#1).

Are you married? _____

Do you have children? _____

If so, how many? _____

If you are married, does your spouse work outside the home? _____

If so, what is your spouse's job? _____

What is your spouse's monthly income?

4. $ [ ]

How much of your spouse's income is withheld for income tax?

5. $ [ ]

What is your spouse's total available income?
To get this figure, subtract the amount in the gray box (#5) from the amount in the top white box (#4).

6. $ [ ]

What is the TOTAL available income for you and your spouse?
To get this figure, add items #3 and #6.

7. $ [ ]

Expenses

A.   Housing

Where do you live? (In a condominium, in your own home, in a rented home, in an apartment, on a farm, in a mobile home, somewhere else?) _____

Describe the size and location of your home. (A modest one-bedroom basement apartment? A five-bedroom home in an upscale suburb? An efficiency apartment in a high-rise, somewhere else?) _____

What is your monthly rent or house payment?

8. $ [ ]

What is your average total monthly utility bill (gas, electric, water, etc.)?

9. $ [ ]

What is your monthly telephone bill? (Remember to add special features like call waiting, conference calling, etc., if you want them. Be sure to remember long distance calls.)

10. $ [ ]

If you own a home, how much do you pay in property tax per month?

11. $ [ ]

What other basic expenses do you have for your home (garbage collection, yard work, etc.)?

12. $ [ ]

B.   Transportation

Do you own a car or cars? _____ If so, how many? _____

What is your total monthly car payment?   **13.** $ [   ]

What is your total monthly car insurance payment?   **14.** $ [   ]

How much do you spend per month on gasoline?   **15.** $ [   ]

How much do you spend per month on car maintenance   **16.** $ [   ]
(oil changes, repairs, tires, tune-ups, etc.)?

If you don't own a car, how much do you spend per month on   **17.** $ [   ]
transportation (bus fares, train fares, bicycle maintenance, etc.)?

C.   Family obligations

Do you need to pay for child care costs? _____

If so, do your children stay in a day care center, a private home or with a relative?

_____

What is your total average child care cost per month?   **18.** $ [   ]

How old are your parents now?   _____

Could one or both be living with you or in a nursing home at this time? _____

If so, who is responsible for paying for their care? _____

If it is likely to be you, what is the monthly cost?   **19.** $ [   ]

D.   Food

How much do you spend per month on groceries?   **20.** $ [   ]

E.   Household and personal basics
                                                                             21.
How much do you spend per month on household and personal $ [   ]
basics (laundry detergent, cleaning products, paper towels,
shampoo, toothpaste, soap, deodorant, cosmetics, etc.)? Think of
every member of your family in determining this cost.

F.   Clothing

What are your average monthly clothing costs? Include every member of your family, and include underwear, diapers, shoes, coats, special sports clothing, dry cleaning bills, etc. (If it's easier, figure out a yearly total for every person's needs. Add them up, and divide by 12.)

22. $ [   ]

G.   Insurance

How much per month do you spend on health insurance? **23.** $ [   ]

Life insurance? **24.** $ [   ]

Property or renter's insurance ? **25.** $ [   ]

H.   Health care

How much do you spend per month on health care — doctor's appointments, braces, glasses, etc.? Remember to include each member of your family .

26. $ [   ]

I.   Entertainment

Do you have cable TV? _____

What is the monthly payment? **27.** $ [   ]

How much per month do you spend on entertainment (movies, video games, video rentals, skiing, eating out, etc.)? **28.** $ [   ]

Do you belong to a health club or any other organizations? _____

What is the total cost, per month? **29.** $ [   ]

Do you subscribe to any magazines, newspapers or other publications? _____

What is the total cost, per month? **30.** $ [   ]

J.   Vacation

Do you travel or take vacations? _____

How many per year? _____

How much does the average vacation cost your family ? _____

What is your monthly travel allowance? To get this figure, add up the total vacation costs and divide by 12. **31.** $ [   ]

K. Emergency

What kinds of unexpected expenses or emergency expenses might come up (the refrigerator breaks, the basement floods, someone in the family is in a car accident, there are funeral expenses for a relative, a pet needs to be spayed, etc.)?

_____

_____

_____

_____

Set up a monthly allowance to go into an emergency fund: **32.** $ _____

L. Savings

How much do you put into a savings account each month? **33.** $ _____

Into a retirement fund? **34.** $ _____

M. Miscellaneous

Do you have pets? _____

What are the average monthly costs for food, vet bills, etc.? **35.** $ _____

Do you contribute to a church, political organization, charity or other group?_____

What is the total cost, per month? **36.** $ _____

Do you give your children an allowance? _____

If so, what is the total cost for all your children, per month? **37.** $ _____

Other expenses not listed above:

_____ **38.** $ _____

_____ **39.** $ _____

_____ **40.** $ _____

_____ **41.** $ _____

_____ **42.** $ _____

_____ **43.** $ _____

_____ **44.** $ _____

_____ **45.** $ _____

Budget Worksheet
for one month

Income

Total available income: $ _____$
(See box #7.)

Expenses

A. Housing

Rent/house
payments   **8.** $ _____

Utilities   **9.** $ _____

Telephone   **10.** $ _____

Property tax   **11.** $ _____

Other basics   **12.** $ _____

TOTAL $ _____

B. Transportation

Car payments   **13.** $ _____

Car insurance   **14.** $ _____

Gasoline   **15.** $ _____

Car
maintenance   **16.** $ _____

Other
transportation   **17.** $ _____

TOTAL $ _____

C. Family obligations

Child care   **18.** $ _____

Aging
parent care   **19.** $ _____

TOTAL $ _____

D. Food

TOTAL   **20.** $ _____

E. Household and personal basics

TOTAL   **21.** $ _____

F. Clothing

TOTAL   **22.** $ _____

G. Insurance

Health
insurance   **23.** $ _____

Life insurance   **24.** $ _____

Property
insurance   **25.** $ _____

TOTAL $ _____

H. Health care

TOTAL   **26.** $_____

I. Entertainment

Cable   **27.** $_____

Entertainment   **28.** $_____

Health club
and other
organizations   **29.** $_____

Magazines, news-
papers and other
publications   **30.** $_____

TOTAL $_____

J. Vacation

TOTAL   **31.** $_____

K. Emergency

TOTAL   **32.** $_____

L. Savings

Savings
account   **33.** $_____

Retirement
fund   **34.** $_____

TOTAL $_____

M. Miscellaneous

Pets   **35.** $_____

Contributions   **36.** $_____

Children's
Allowance   **37.** $_____

Other expenses
(See boxes #38-45.) $_____

TOTAL $_____

* * * * * * * * * * * * * * * * * *

What is your total available income? (See box #7.)   **TOTAL** $_____

Add all the boxed totals, items A–M. This is the total monthly expenses for your household.   **TOTAL** $_____

Now subtract your total monthly expense from your total available income. The result is the amount of money you have left at the end of the month after expenses.   **TOTAL** $_____

How are you doing? Do you have enough money for expenses? If not, where can you adjust? How can you make ends meet?

I'll NEVER need this stuff!

Be bold in what you stand for and careful what you fall for.

Ruth Boorstin

Young people sometimes joke that mothers and fathers everywhere must have a book they consult on parenthood. They all learn to say things like, "I don't care if everybody else is going. If everybody else was jumping off a cliff, would you jump off, too?" Or "Get off that phone. Now!" Or "If I have to stop this car, you're going to wish I hadn't." Or the classic, "Because I said so."

Teachers sometimes joke that students have the same kind of book, only with a list of things that students should say in class. Teachers hear lines like these over and over again:

- This is dumb. I'll never need to know this stuff.
- Why do I have to know how to write? I'm never going to be an English teacher. (Or why do I have to know geometry? I'm going to be an English teacher.)
- Why do we have to study this stuff? It's boring.

Have you ever made any of the above statements, or similar ones? If so, there was some truth in what you were saying. It's absolutely true that you *may* never need to know about something you are studying in school.

However, there is also the possibility that you may. You just don't know. You may *think* you know. You may even be right. But you could very well be wrong.

Let's look at it another way. Can you foresee the future? Can you guess everything that's going to happen to you in your life? Do you know how the world is going to change over the next ten or twenty years, or the next thirty or forty years, or the next fifty or sixty years?

Of course not. That's why you should read the following true stories about real people — real people who were no better at predicting the future than you are.

Henry, farmer

Henry is 68 years old. The son of a German immigrant, he grew up on a farm and always knew that he wanted to grow up and become a farmer. His teachers knew it, too, and even though he was a good student, one told him: "You don't need to go past eighth grade. You're going to be a farmer, and you won't really need a high school education." So, after eighth grade, Henry dropped out of school.

Henry *did* grow up and become a farmer, and he was a good one. He also got married and had four children. Then one year there was a terrible hailstorm, and all the crops were wiped out just before harvest time. He managed to hang on through the next year. Then the same thing happened again. Again, he was wiped out. There was no question — he had to get a job to support his family during the winter.

That was easier said than done. He had only an eighth grade education, and most jobs required more schooling. The only job he could get was as a low-paid factory worker in a sugar beet factory. He hated the job, but there was little he could do. Because he hadn't gone past the eighth grade, he had few choices.

Sue, business owner

"I hate algebra," Sue used to complain in junior high. "I know I'm going to grow up and be a teacher — and not a math teacher. When am I ever going to need algebra?"

Sue did grow up to be a teacher. After many years, she decided to change careers. She started her own business and now has to handle the financial management of her company. "I use algebra all the time now," she says. "But when I was 14 I would have bet everything I owned that I would NEVER EVER use algebra again in my life. You just never know."

Bradley, 22-year-old father of four

"I'll never need this stuff!" said Bradley all the time. "I know I'm going to go to the police academy and become a policeman. I don't need to know anything about math or science or English."

At 19 he fell in love with a woman who already had one small child, and he married her. They quickly had another baby and then twins. Bradley applied to the police academy and didn't get in. He tried to get in the army, but his scores were too low. Now he has four children and can't get a job that pays much above minimum wage. He is a bright young man, but his basic knowledge skills are too low to get him into the kind of work he would like to do.

In the meantime, he has four kids, something he never ever would have guessed he would have at age 22.

Devona, frustrated occupational therapist

Devona hated science. In high school she skipped chemistry, physics and biology. She thought her life was complete without knowing the minute details of a cell or a protozoa.

Because of a part-time job she had, Devona later decided she wanted to become an occupational therapist and work with people with disabilities. When she went to college, however, she struggled a lot in her science classes. She almost flunked biology, due in part to the fact that she had never learned to do a lab write-up in high school.

The result? She didn't have the grades to get into the occupational therapy program. "Even though I was really good at working with people with disabilities and had lots of experience," Devona said, "I couldn't become an occupational therapist. I had to change my career goals because I decided too early what classes I needed and didn't need."

Chris, ski bum

Chris dropped out of high school. He insisted that it was all a waste of time. He studied for the General Educational Development (GED) test and passed. Then he moved to the mountains to work in a ski shop and ski during the winter.

He made lots of friends and was a great worker. However, he often found himself in awkward situations. People would start discussing something in the news, and his lack of knowledge about history and geography would show up. Friends would bring out a game like "Trivial Pursuit" at a party, and he would joke a lot to cover up how few of the answers he knew. He would join a discussion, and his poor vocabulary meant he couldn't quite follow what some people were saying.

Chris finds himself hiding the fact that he doesn't have a high school diploma. He is working to get into a college. He will make it, but he sees already that it is going to be hard to make up for all he missed in high school.

Tammy, part-time waitress

Tammy always hated school and said she didn't need it. "I'm going to own my own restaurant," she said. "And I'm going to marry a rich man." After high school, she moved to a city and started working at a restaurant to learn the ropes. However, she didn't even earn minimum wage and certainly couldn't save enough to buy a restaurant on her own. She also found she wasn't even *meeting* any rich men, let alone finding one to marry.

Last year Tammy had to move back home to live with her father. She wasn't making enough money to live on her own and she was deeply in debt. Bill collectors are hounding her, but she can't find any work she is qualified for, except a job as a part-time waitress. She is miserable and says she can see no future for herself.

Collecting real-life stories

Talk to at least two adults you know, and share one or more of the stories above. Then find out their answers to the following questions:

- Do you have a similar story you could tell? If so, what is it?
- Can you think of something you wish you had paid more attention to in school? Why?
- Have you ever found yourself using something you learned in school more than you ever thought you would? If so, what is it?
- If you were going to school all over again, what would you do differently? Why?
- Is there something you are very glad you studied in school? Explain.
- Looking back, what do you think was most important about school? Why?

A Perfect Day in the Future

Go confidently in the direction of your dreams! Live the life you've imagined.

Henry David Thoreau

I simply imagine it so, then go about to prove it.

Albert Einstein

Your ideal day

People have probably been telling you all your life that school can help you secure a better future for yourself. However, sometimes it is hard to imagine the future. It is important to stop every now and then and try to see the future as we would like it to be.

Think ahead 15-20 years and imagine what your ideal day might be like. Imagine a typical day, not a day off, a vacation day or a holiday. Since most people have to work, include your job as part of the day.

In writing about your perfect day, be sure to include plenty of details. For example, if you write that you wake up at noon, explain *why* you are able to wake up at noon. ("I wake up at noon because I work nights at my celebrity night club in New York City.")

Here's an example of one student's ideal day:

> *I wake up at 7:00 and eat some chocolate Pop-Tarts. After I get ready for work, I get on my motorcycle and ride to downtown Phoenix, Arizona. I have to open my own motorcycle shop at 9:00 a.m. In the morning, I work on fixing up some classic bikes. I was hired by Harley Davidson to fix these bikes up for its national museum in Sturgis, South Dakota. I have someone to do small repairs and work the front of the store in the morning.*
>
> *At noon I eat some leftovers from last night's dinner that I made. (I love to cook and have become so good at it that I don't like to eat anyone else's cooking.) In the afternoon I work in the store front so I can meet people. I get to meet a lot of cool people that way. I close my shop up around 5:00 and ride my bike home.*
>
> *Once home, I fix dinner before my son gets home from baseball practice (He's the star player on his Little League team) and before my wife gets home from her modeling shoot. After dinner, my wife cleans up the dinner mess while I help my son with his homework. Later, my wife and I swap stories about our days and watch the evening news. After that I go to bed and sleep until my next ideal day.*

Categories

After you have completed writing, divide the important items from your ideal day into the following categories:

- **Need-to-have.** These are the items you think are absolutely necessary for your ideal day.
- **Want-to-have.** These are the items that you really want but that you could live without if you had to.
- **Super bonus extras.** These are fringe benefits, the extras that would help make life perfect.

Here's how the student above divided his items:

Need-to-have	*Want-to-have*	*Super bonus extras*
• *a motorcycle*	• *to be a good cook*	• *a wife who is a fashion model*
• *a motorcycle shop*	• *to have an employee at my shop*	• *being able to work for the Harley Davidson museum*
• *a family*	• *to have a wife who will clean up my cooking messes*	• *a son who is good at baseball*
• *to live in a warm place like Phoenix*	• *to have a son*	

Reaching your goals

Now, write down five steps that will help you to attain the things in your *need-to-have* list. Here are the steps the student above chose:

- Go to mechanics school after high school.
- Take some business classes at the local community college to learn how to keep my books.
- Work and save my money to be able to buy a motorcycle.
- Pay my bills on time so I have good credit. That will help me get a loan to set up my shop.
- Work for two years under the supervision of a motorcycle specialist.
- Get my shop established before I have kids, so I'll be able to support them.

After you have completed your steps, share them with four other people, including at least two adults. Is there anything important you may have forgotten to include? Revise your steps, if necessary.

Now, save your list and look at it from time to time. Feel free to adjust it as your goals change over the years. Having a picture of your ideal day will help you create the life you want for yourself, especially if you work to follow the steps necessary to reach your goals.

Making Life ➡ Connections

If you can walk, you can dance. If you can talk, you can sing.
— Saying from Zimbabwe

- What do fractions have to do with real life?
- Why do I have to learn to spell?
- Why do I need to know about the Civil War?

Have you ever found yourself asking questions like these? Sometimes it's hard to see connections between school and real life. There *are* connections, though.

Sometimes the connections are pretty obvious. It's easy to see that knowing how to spell can make it easier to communicate with others. Sometimes the connections are less obvious. It's harder to see that studying geometry can help you learn to think logically, or that studying chemistry can help develop your memory, or that studying *anything* will help you learn self-discipline.

Below are a number of topics that students study in school. See if you can think of five ways each of them might be used in real life. Feel free to get suggestions from adults, other relatives, neighbors, teachers or anyone else you know who can help you. Remember — someone older can sometimes see a use that might not occur to you, simply because that person has been around longer. Don't be afraid to ask.

Real-life uses for fractions

1. Doubling a chocolate chip cookie recipe

2. Knowing how much 1/3 off will be on a shirt from the sale rack

3. _____

4. _____

5. _____

6. _____

7. _____

Real-life uses for speech

1. Performing well during a job interview

2. Giving your side of a dispute in court

3. _____

4. _____

5. _____

6. _____

7. _____

Real-life uses for science

1. Knowing how to test a hypothesis in your job

2. Figuring out why your rose bush is dying

3. _____

4. _____

5. _____

6. _____

7. _____

Real-life uses for multiplication and division

1. Figuring out how much a wedding dinner for 95 people will cost, at $12.95 per plate

2. Determining how many square feet of carpeting to order for your dining room

3. _____

4. _____

5. _____

6. _____

7. _____

Real-life uses for reading

1. Understanding people better

2. Having something to do when you are waiting at an airport

3. _____

4. _____

5. _____

6. _____

7. _____

Real-life uses for writing

1. Creating an effective job resume

2. Getting results when you have a complaint with a business

3. _____

4. _____

5. _____

6. _____

7. _____

Real-life uses for history

1. Knowing about the Bill of Rights and the Constitution, so that no one tries to take away your rights illegally

2. Understanding what your great grandfather means when he talks about "The Crash"

3. _____

4. _____

5. _____

6. _____

7. _____

Real-life uses for PE

1. Knowing how to work as part of a team

2. Learning sports that will help you stay fit throughout your life

3. _____

4. _____

5. _____

6. _____

7. _____

Real-life uses for _____ (You list the school subject or topic.)

1. _____

2. _____

3. _____

4. _____

5. _____

Real-life uses for_____ (You list the school subject or topic.)

1. _____

2. _____

3. _____

4. _____

5. _____

Real-life uses for_____ (You list the school subject or topic.)

1. _____

2. _____

3. _____

4. _____

5. _____

Making Life ➡ Connections

Answer Key

Answers will vary.

Real-life uses for fractions

3. Knowing how much a ¼¢ tax will increase the price of goods
4. Figuring how to split a pie evenly for eight people
5. Understanding what portion of your tax dollar is going to defense, education, the environment, etc.
6. Determining how much fabric you need to make a shirt
7. Figuring your favorite baseball player's batting average

Real-life uses for speech

3. Calling businesses for information
4. Demanding a refund for a defective product
5. Giving your opinion to the city council on a new housing development
6. Proposing a toast at your brother's wedding
7. Presenting a new idea to your boss

Real-life uses for science

3. Being able to tell what type of clouds mean bad weather
4. Identifying planets in a night sky
5. Knowing which household cleaners, when combined, will emit a poisonous gas
6. Understanding what your doctor says
7. Knowing which berries and plants are safe to eat when hiking

Real-life uses for multiplication and division

3. Figuring out how long it will take to save money for a dirt bike
4. Figuring your gas mileage
5. Determining how many gallons of paint you need to paint your house
6. Figuring how much it would cost for your whole family to go to Disneyland
7. Dividing the electric bill, telephone bill, cable bill, etc., with your roommate

Real-life uses for reading

3. Being able to follow instructions in a manual
4. Understanding common literary references made on TV, in music, by politicians, etc.
5. Getting more in-depth information about current events than TV and videos can provide
6. Being able to use the library as a free source of information
7. Figuring out what's in a contract before you sign it

Real-life uses for writing

3. Writing a clear, concise memo to promote an idea to your boss
4. Leaving instructions for your house-sitter
5. Writing a letter to your elected representative to voice your opinion on certain issues
6. Writing advertisement copy that sells your product
7. Composing a letter to the editor of your local paper

Real-life uses for history

3. Understanding historical references in books, movies, etc.
4. Making an informed decision when joining a political party
5. Understanding the culture and history when you visit another country
6. Understanding the historical context of current events
7. Understanding your ethnic background and traditions

Real-life uses for PE

3. Joining a bowling team to meet people in a new town
4. Knowing what is going on when watching a game or match
5. Having something to do on Saturday afternoon
6. Coaching your child's Little League team
7. Knowing how to stretch properly so you don't pull a muscle or get shin splints

Teacher Instructions
for

AND THE JOB GOES TO . . .

You're HIRED!

Would You Hire You?

The next three activities help students look ahead to the real-life world of work. "And the Job Goes to . . ." is a short play to read aloud in class. It helps students see the relationship between school and the future, from the point of view of employers. For a follow-up to the play, you might ask several employers to come and talk to your students about what they look for in employees, and about what *they* see as the connection between school and work. What do they wish employees had paid more attention to in school? What skills are most helpful for employees at their business? (It's a good idea to choose employers from both low-paying and high-paying jobs.)

"You're Hired!" has students play the role of personnel manager. Based on letters from three job applicants, they choose the candidate they would hire for the job of management trainee, based on the president of the company's requirements. Most students will quickly eliminate the first candidate, for a variety of reasons, but the choice between the remaining two candidates is difficult. There are arguments for hiring either one of them, and students must think carefully to defend their choices in a memo to the president. (Which applicant is most likely to stay with the company? Does working as a cashier indicate more or less responsibility than taking care of a younger brother and sister?)

Finally — after students have completed "And the Job Goes to . . ." and "You're Hired!" — they evaluate themselves with "Would You Hire You?" You may want to discuss the activity with students before they write, pointing out that they might hire themselves for some jobs and not for others. Which jobs would they be most suited for? Which ones would not be a good match? Ask students to explain how they might view themselves if they were in the shoes of an employer.

aND THe JOB GOeS TO ...

*Every morning I get up and look through the Forbes list of the richest people in America.
If I'm not there, I go to work.*

— Robert Orben

Read aloud the short play below:

List of Characters:

Mrs. Black, a teacher
Jared, a junior in high school
Mr. Montoya, an employer
Ms. Palucci, an employer
Ms. Cornwall, an employer
Mr. Jones, an employer

Mrs. Black:	Jared, you need to bring your grades up. I'm concerned about you.
Jared:	Don't be concerned about me. I don't care about my grades. Why should you?
Mrs. Black:	Because you are going to graduate next year.
Jared:	So what? I'm not going to college. I'm just going to get a job, and my boss sure isn't going to care about how I did in earth science.
Mrs. Black:	True — if you're lucky. Some bosses don't care. But a lot of them do, especially the ones who offer better jobs.
Jared:	That's not fair. My schoolwork doesn't have anything to do with working in an electronics factory or an oil-changing place.
Mr. Montoya:	Wrong.
	(Suddenly Jared is surrounded by 5 adults. He looks around, puzzled.)
Jared:	Who are you? Is this a dream or what?
Mr. Montoya:	No, it's not a dream. It's a reality check. I'm Joe Montoya, and I own a Quickie Lube downtown. I think how you do in earth science does have something to do with how you will do changing oil.
Jared:	Oh sure. Like how?

Mr. Montoya:	Well, when somebody is doing poorly in school, tardies and absences are often a factor. I don't want an employee who is going to use any excuse in the world to be gone or who will come in late. So I *do* look at school records when I'm hiring a student or someone just out of school.
Ms. Palucci:	So do I.
Jared:	Great. It's a conspiracy.
Ms. Palucci:	No, it's just the truth. I look at grades, too. Sometimes kids are rotten students because they have a bad attitude. I don't want to deal with that. I'm paying somebody, so I don't want to have any hassles with them.
Jared:	Well, I may get into trouble a lot in school, but I'll know how to behave on the job.
Ms. Palucci:	Maybe. But I doubt it. It's pretty hard to change your behavior overnight. There are exceptions, but I've found that kids who are mouthy at school are mouthy on the job.
Jared:	So are you trying to say I'll never get a job if I have rotten grades or get in trouble in school?
Ms. Cornwall:	Nope. You could get a job from me.
Jared:	Great! What do you do?
Ms. Cornwall:	I own a fast food franchise. Frankly, I need so many workers that I have trouble keeping enough help.
Jared:	(Triumphantly) See? So I'll work there!
Mr. Montoya:	Why do you have trouble keeping enough help? What happens to the employees?
Ms. Cornwall:	Oh, they're always quitting.
Mr. Montoya:	Why?
Ms. Cornwall:	Because I don't pay very much. Most kids can never earn much more than minimum wage, even if they are really good. There's not a whole lot of chance for advancement here.
Mr. Jones:	People can advance in my business.
Jared:	And what's that?
Mr. Jones:	I own a sporting goods store. I like to hire people with lots of skills, people who are likely to advance in the business. Someone who can run a cash register is fine. But if that person can run a cash register, knows basic bookkeeping skills, can express herself really well, and knows how to deal with people, she might become a manager. That kind of person is really valuable.

Jared:	(Stubbornly) I would never want to be a manager anyway. I don't want to be in charge of anything. I just want a good job working for someone else who makes the decisions.
Mr. Montoya:	Well, you probably wouldn't work for me. I have found that people who do well in school know how to organize their time and how to follow instructions. They are probably dependable. They fit in.
Mr. Jones:	And the ones who don't do well in school often have poor basic skills. I don't want somebody working for me who can't add and subtract or read very well.
Jared:	Oh, like you really need to read well to sell somebody a pair of sneakers!
Mr. Jones:	Maybe not. But things come up all the time. Suppose the computer breaks down, and I need someone to study an instruction book to find out what went wrong? Or suppose someone needs to calculate quickly whether or not a delivery invoice from a supplier is correct? There are always needs for people with good basic skills.
Ms. Cornwall:	I think the main point is that good students have shown that they can do one job well — going to school. People who do one job well can often do another well.
Jared:	That's ridiculous. My friend Blake was a terrible student. Now he's doing real well at the big discount distribution warehouse, where he's working on the loading dock.
Mr. Jones:	Good for Blake. There are always Blakes around who prove the exception to the rule. I hope you turn out to be a Blake.
Jared:	I will. You just wait and see.

What do you think? What kind of job do you think Jared will get? How will he do? What do you think the future holds for him? Explain.

_____

_____

_____

_____

_____

_____

_____

You're HIRED!

Success is getting what you want, and happiness is wanting what you get.
— Dave Gardner

You are the personnel manager of a rapidly growing widget company called the Precision Widget Company. You have a position open for a management trainee.

The president of the company, Walt Widget, wants someone **smart, responsible** and **willing to learn the business**. He also wants someone who is likely to **stay with the company.**

Mr. Widget has given you three letters. Based on these three letters you must decide which person to hire.

Here are the three letters:

Letter 1:

To the person in charge:

I'm lookin for a Job for awhile to make some Money and I heard you guys pay real good. I want to buy a Car and have money to hang out with my friends and stuff.

I'm pretty smart, but my teachers always give me a hard time cuz school's a drag. I hope I can come in at about 10 or 11 to work so I can get some sleep cuz we hang out and stuff and I don't usually get to Bed until late.

See ya,
Marissa Gladstone

Letter 2:

Dear Hiring Manager:

I would like to work for the Precision Widget Company. I am a hard worker and have a B-average.

I don't have too much experience, because I have to be home to watch my baby brother and sister when my mom goes to work at night. I help my mom with all the household chores and am pretty good at fixing things around the house. The neighbors have hired me to mow their lawn on the weekends and I like doing a good job for them.

I can work full-time during the days. I like learning and want to learn more about making widgets. If I get this job, it will help me save some money to take some part-time classes at night at Riverside Community College. I could take some classes about widget making maybe.

Thank you,
Franklin Spence

Letter 3:

Dear Personnel:

    I would like to apply for a position with the Semi-Accurate Precision Widget Company. I am always on time and willing to learn new skills. I am also a hard worker.

    I do well in school and have a B average. I play clarinet in the band and play on the soccer team.

    I have been working summers at Barney's Garage for the past two years as a cashier. Barney is retiring and closing his garage, so I am looking for a new job.

    I would really like to work for your company. I would like to go to college and major in business, so I'm trying to make some money to help with tuition.

    I hope I can come to work for you.

Thank you,
Allison Somerville

For discussion and consideration

Mr. Widget is looking for some specific qualities in his new employee. Review those qualities (in italics at the beginning of the activity), and then consider each of the candidates:

1. Would Marissa Gladstone be a good candidate for this job? Why or why not? Does she meet the qualifications? What do you see as her strengths?

2. Would Franklin Spence be a good candidate for this job? Why or why not? Does he meet the qualifications? What do you see as his strengths?

3. Would Allison Somerville be a good candidate for this job? Why or why not? Does she meet the qualifications? What do you see as her strengths?

4. Now, you have to make a decision. Who are you going to hire? Why? You must justify your decision to the company president in the memo that follows.

MEMO

TO: Walt Widget, President

FROM: _____ , Personnel Manager

RE: Hiring of new management trainee

I have hired the following person for the position: _____

The five reasons why I decided to hire this person are:

1.

2.

3.

4.

5.

Name _____

Would You Hire You?

Work is much more fun than fun.

— Noel Coward

If you were an employer, would you hire *you* for a job? Why or why not? Explain.
(Some things to consider: What good qualities do you have? What experience do you have?
Are you reliable? Would you fit some jobs better than others? Why?)

_____
_____
_____
_____
_____
_____
_____
_____
_____
_____
_____
_____
_____
_____
_____
_____
_____
_____
_____

Advantages of Being a Good Student

You have brains in your head.
You have feet in your shoes.
You can steer yourself any direction you choose.

— Dr. Seuss

There are some obvious advantages to being a good student. You are eligible for scholarships, for example, and you never get grounded for having bad grades.

But there are also a lot of less obvious awards. Here are just a few of them:

- Your grandma tells people how proud she is of you.

- Your parents never nag you about trying harder.

- When you get a driver's license, you may be able to get a "good student" discount on your insurance.

- You can get a bad grade once in awhile and your parents understand.

- You get away with more. No one suspects a good student.

See if you can think of at least 10 more advantages to being a good student. Remember, they don't have to be *big* advantages. You can include small advantages as well!

1. _____

2. _____

3. _____

4. _____

5. _____

6. _____

7. _____

8. _____

9. _____

10. _____

Building on STRENGTHS

Building on Strengths

This chapter is designed to help students take a close look at themselves. The activities help them determine their strengths and learn to build on those strengths.

If you are going to try just one activity in this section with your students, the one not to miss is "What are You Good At?" (page 55). If you simply ask students what they are good at, they will often mumble, "Oh, nothing," or "Nothing much." This activity, however, tries a different approach. Students receive a list of over 300 things that a person can be good at, and they simply need to check any that apply to them.

For most, dozens and dozens apply. Students often start smiling to themselves as they go through the list, surprised at how many items they are circling. Then it is easier for them to go on and write down other strengths that aren't even on the list. The activity provides an excellent, non-threatening way for students to acknowledge what they have going for themselves.

Name _____

WHO ARE YOU?

Tell me what you pay attention to and I will tell you who you are.

Jose Ortega y Gasset

Who are you, really? Maybe you're not the person your friends think you are, or your parents think you are, or your teachers think you are. Maybe you're not even the person *you* think you are.

For example, Josie thinks she is not very smart. True, she doesn't get good grades in school, but she reads constantly and knows much more than most people her age about nearly every subject imaginable. She *is* smart, but because of her grades, she thinks of herself as less than intelligent.

Sometimes we don't know very much about the people we should know best of all — ourselves. Take a look at yourself by completing the following sentences in as many ways as possible. Don't think terribly hard. Just write down the first answers that occur to you.

I get excited when . . .

_____

_____

I get teary-eyed and choked up when . . .

_____

_____

I feel really good about myself when . . .

_____

_____

Time flies when . . .

_____

_____

I really admire . . .

_____

_____

I would like to make a difference in the world by . . .

_____

_____

Look at your list often and hang on to it for a week. Try to add to it each day.

Name _____

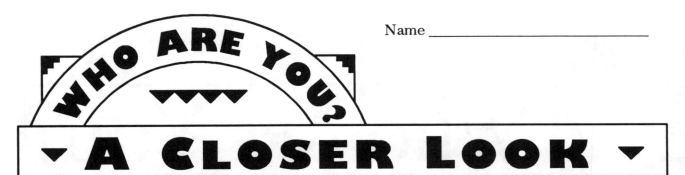

Cherish forever what makes you unique, 'cuz you're really a yawn if it goes!

Bette Midler

Take a good hard look at the "Who are you?" list you completed last week. Things you wrote down are things that you care about, things that affect you deeply. They are the things that make you who you are.

A look at yourself

• Imagine that your list was written by someone else. What can you tell about the person by looking at his or her answers? Describe the person as if you were writing about someone other than yourself.

_____

_____

_____

_____

_____

_____

_____

_____

_____

• Did anything surprise you about the way you completed your list? If so, what? Explain.

_____

_____

_____

_____

_____

_____

WHAT ARE YOU GOOD AT?

Many individuals have, like uncut diamonds, shining qualities beneath a rough exterior.

— Juvenal

Often students don't do as well as they could in school because they have a low opinion of themselves. Though they try to cover it up, they think, "Why bother? I'm no good at anything." What they don't realize is that everyone is good at many things. If you recognize what you are good at, it is easier to build on your strengths.

What are you good at? Many students answer, "Oh, nothing" or "Not much." They don't realize that there are probably dozens and dozens of things they are good at, things they may never even have recognized.

The strengths we have are often the ones we give ourselves the least credit for. If someone can't draw, she will think of drawing as a great talent that she doesn't have. But she won't give herself credit for a talent she *does* have, like the ability to play the saxophone. If someone makes friends easily, he won't recognize that as a strength. Instead he will worry about how easily he gets tongue-tied around girls.

What are you good at? Take a look at yourself and make your own personal list of strengths. Don't forget all the little things you are good at and probably don't even think about.

To help you get started thinking, here is a list of over three hundred talents, large and small. Which ones apply to you? Check all the ones that apply to you, and then add as many more as you can think of. Remember, you can be good at something without having to be an expert.

1. accepting an apology graciously
2. acting in plays
3. adding long columns of numbers correctly without a calculator
4. administering first aid
5. apologizing when you are wrong
6. arranging flowers in a vase
7. baby-sitting
8. backpacking
9. baking cookies
10. being "cool"
11. being coordinated
12. being in a good mood most of the time
13. being nice to people everyone else laughs at
14. being patient with children
15. being responsible
16. being sensitive to other people's feelings
17. being the center of attention
18. being unique
19. bench-pressing your weight
20. blowing bubbles
21. bowling
22. braiding hair
23. building things with your hands

24. calling businesses to find out information
25. camping
26. changing a tire
27. cheering people up
28. cheerleading
29. chilling out
30. choosing good books to read by just looking at the cover
31. choosing good friends
32. cleaning up the kitchen
33. collecting baseball cards
34. coloring inside the lines
35. comforting someone who is sad
36. coming up with creative excuses for not doing something
37. coming up with good Halloween costumes
38. competing in rodeo events
39. completing crossword puzzles
40. complimenting other people
41. computer programming
42. concentrating
43. cooking
44. cooking over a wood stove or campfire
45. correctly predicting who will win a game
46. creating smoothies and shakes
47. crocheting
48. cutting hair
49. dancing
50. daydreaming
51. dealing with emergencies
52. decorating birthday cakes
53. delivering newspapers so they hit the front door with one toss
54. designing holiday decorations
55. diving
56. doing "wheelies" on your bike
57. doing calligraphy
58. doing cartwheels
59. doing gymnastics
60. doing long division
61. doing math problems in your head
62. doing needlepoint
63. doing pantomime
64. doing pull-ups
65. doing push-ups
66. doing tai-kwon-do
67. doing the splits
68. doing two things at once
69. doing well on tests
70. doing your homework, without your parents making you
71. drawing caricatures of people
72. drawing cartoons
73. dreaming up ways to make money
74. driving a boat
75. driving a tractor
76. eating healthy food
77. eating only one potato chip
78. executing karate kicks
79. exercising on a regular basis
80. figuring out a bus schedule
81. figuring out the change you'll get from a store
82. finding bargains
83. finding things in the library
84. finding things that are lost
85. finding your way anywhere on a subway or bus
86. fishing
87. fixing cars
88. fixing flat tires on bicycles
89. flossing every day
90. folding laundry
91. following rules
92. gardening
93. getting along with others
94. getting along with teachers
95. getting away with things
96. getting grandparents to tell interesting stories

97. getting into your house when you're locked out

98. getting jobs

99. getting others to talk about themselves

100. getting people to trust you

101. getting the opposite sex to like you

102. getting the remote control first

103. getting your own way

104. giving directions to lost drivers

105. giving good advice

106. giving manicures

107. going backwards on ice skates

108. grooming a horse

109. growing long fingernails that don't break

110. growing plants

111. guessing the correct time when there's no clock around

112. helping new kids feel welcome at school

113. helping out around the house

114. hemming pants and skirts

115. hiking

116. hitting home runs

117. horseback riding

118. ice skating

119. identifying different types of birds

120. identifying trees and plants

121. imitating the mannerisms of people you know

122. imitating the Three Stooges

123. imitating voices of cartoon characters

124. ironing clothes

125. joking around

126. juggling

127. jumping over obstacles while on a skateboard

128. jumping rope

129. kayaking

130. keeping photos in albums instead of all over the place

131. keeping promises

132. keeping up on current events

133. keeping your room neat

134. knitting

135. knowing all of the state capitals

136. knowing how to avoid dangerous parts of your neighborhood

137. knowing the names of all NFL quarterbacks

138. knowing what people are thinking

139. knowing when to say "no"

140. knowing where people come from by hearing their accents

141. laughing

142. learning a foreign language

143. learning the words to songs on the radio

144. line dancing

145. lip-synching to CDs

146. listening

147. loading the dishwasher so a lot fits in

148. making "fun" messages for answering machines

149. making a baby stop crying

150. making a house out of a deck of cards

151. making an omelet

152. making animal noises

153. making authentic "burb" sounds

154. making balloon animals

155. making banana splits

156. making brownies from scratch

157. making colorful designs with markers

158. making delicious sandwiches

159. making friends

160. making homemade greeting cards

161. making paper airplanes that fly far

162. making people laugh

163. making perfect popcorn, without a microwave oven

164. making pottery

165. making snow forts
166. making spaghetti
167. making up dances
168. making up new recipes
169. making up songs
170. making up stories
171. making your grandparents happy
172. mashing potatoes without any lumps
173. meeting deadlines
174. memorizing things
175. milking a cow
176. minding your manners
177. mountain biking
178. mountain climbing
179. mowing lawns
180. multiplying fractions
181. naming pets
182. noticing what you are good at
183. operating a calculator
184. ordering the best thing on the menu at a restaurant
185. organizing parties
186. painting walls without spilling paint on the carpet
187. painting with watercolors or oils
188. paying back what you owe
189. peeling apples by making one long peel
190. performing magic tricks

191. petting cats to get them to purr
192. picking out gifts that people really like
193. picking out great-tasting melons
194. picking the fastest line
195. planning things for you and your friends to do
196. planning things to do in the car on long trips, so no one gets bored
197. playing "pretend" games with children
198. playing a musical instrument
199. playing baseball
200. playing basketball
201. playing card games
202. playing chess
203. playing football
204. playing golf
205. playing miniature golf
206. playing Pictionary
207. playing racquetball
208. playing Scrabble
209. playing soccer
210. playing tennis
211. playing video games
212. playing volleyball
213. protecting your friends
214. putting models together
215. putting on make-up
216. putting together jigsaw puzzles

217. putting together outfits that look great
218. quoting the good lines from a favorite movie
219. reading books, even in the summer
220. reading fast
221. reading magazines from cover to cover
222. reading out loud
223. reading the bottom line on an eye chart
224. reading to children
225. recognizing the constellations in the night sky
226. recycling
227. remembering all the episodes of "The Brady Bunch" reruns
228. remembering birthdays
229. remembering directions for how to get somewhere
230. remembering people's names
231. remembering to floss your teeth
232. remembering what time TV shows are on
233. remembering when assignments are due
234. remembering your dreams
235. rhyming
236. riding a bicycle with no hands
237. rock climbing
238. Rollerblading

239. roller-skating
240. rubbing your stomach and patting your head at the same time
241. running fast
242. running the bases in baseball
243. saving money
244. scuba diving
245. seeing the best in people
246. seeing the good in a bad situation
247. selling for fund-raisers
248. setting a table correctly
249. sewing
250. shooting free throws
251. shooting pool
252. shooting videos
253. singing
254. skateboarding
255. skiing
256. snow boarding
257. solving problems
258. speaking in front of a group of people
259. spelling
260. spiking a volleyball
261. square-dancing
262. standing on your head
263. staying out of trouble
264. steering a toboggan
265. sticking up for the underdog
266. sticking up for yourself
267. styling hair
268. surfing
269. surfing the Internet
270. swimming
271. swimming laps without getting a side ache
272. taking care of pets
273. taking care of yourself
274. taking photographs
275. talking on the phone
276. talking to people you have just met
277. tap dancing
278. teaching cats tricks
279. teaching children how to do things
280. telling jokes
281. telling stories
282. thinking up things to do in the summer
283. throwing a fast ball
284. throwing snowballs
285. touching your toes
286. trimming a Christmas tree
287. typing fast on a computer keyboard
288. understanding people's body language
289. understanding the meaning of big words
290. using a computer
291. using big words occasionally
292. walking the dog
293. washing cars
294. washing the dog
295. water skiing
296. winning
297. wrapping presents
298. wrestling
299. writing notes to friends
300. writing with either hand

A LOOK AT WHAT YOU ARE GOOD AT

Do not let what you cannot do interfere with what you can do.

— John Wooden

When you know what you are good at, you can build on your strengths.

Ross, for example, hates school, but he loves downhill skiing more than anything in the world. Sometimes he is able to tap into that interest in order to do better in school. When he had to write a research paper, he chose to write about Olympic ski champions. Because he was so interested in the subject, he was able to write a better paper than he might have otherwise. He is also very good at telling funny stories. He signed up for a speech class instead of an art class as an elective. Now he can often use humor in his speeches.

Ross is far from a straight-A student, but building on his strengths is helping him do better in school.

Take a closer look at your strengths:

• Copy down all the items you marked in "What are you good at?" Be sure to include all the items you added to the list.

• Beside each item you are good at, write a *quality* that the skill suggests. For example, if you marked that you are good at getting into the house when you are locked out, that might show the qualities of resourcefulness or imagination. If you are good at complimenting others, that might show the qualities of kindness or sensitivity to others.

   This is not an easy task to complete. You may want to consult others for help when you get stuck. (A thesaurus can also be very helpful.)

• Brainstorm ways you could build on your strengths. How could you use them to do better in school? (If you are good at gardening, you could do a science fair project that involves plants. If you are good at helping out the underdog, you could build on that strength by working as a team leader on a class project, helping someone in the group who isn't doing so well.)

   In brainstorming ideas, remember to look at both the specific thing you are good at and at the *quality* it suggests. For example, suppose you are good at doing karate kicks, but you can't figure out how doing karate kicks can help you in school. Look at the quality it suggests and see that learning karate shows self-discipline. You could use self-discipline to try harder to learn how to multiply improper fractions.

A word picture of the
ME I'd like to BE

As long as you can envision the fact that you can do something, you can do it.

Arnold Schwarzenegger

Many athletes today recognize the value of picturing themselves accomplishing certain goals. For example, a swimmer might imagine herself breaking the women's freestyle record. A baseball player might imagine himself pitching a no-hitter. A skater might imagine herself executing a perfect triple axle.

The same technique can help people accomplish other goals. A salesman might imagine the new car he will buy when he meets his sales goal. A smoker who wants to quit may imagine herself getting through the day without going outside for a cigarette. An actor auditioning for a role may imagine himself getting the lead and performing to rave reviews.

How about you and your goals? Are you exactly the person you would like to be in every way? What would you like to change? How would you *like* to be?

Creating a word picture of the perfect you

Make a word collage of the perfect you. Here's how:

- Go through old magazines and newspapers. Cut out words that describe the way you would like to be.

  Also cut out words to describe all the things you already like about yourself. (Don't be modest. No one but you has to know which words describe the present you and which describe the perfect you.)

- If there are words you can't find anywhere, write them yourself in various sizes and colors. Or use a computer, calligraphy, a stencil or press-on letters.

- Arrange all your words in a design that appeals to you, and paste them into a collage. (You may want to include photographs or drawings, too.)

- Give the collage a title that appeals to you. (Just a few ideas: "The Perfect Me," "The Me I Want to Be," "The Future Me," "The Perfect Tyrone Smith")

Now hang your collage where you will see it frequently — perhaps in your room or in your locker. Whenever you look at it, be glad about being the person you already are. Imagine becoming even more of the person you would like to be.

Teacher Instructions
for
The One and Only YOU

The three "The One and Only You" activities that follow are designed to help students see that people learn in different ways, and that it is important for a person to understand how he or she functions best. The activities are *not* intended to be a formal evaluation of learning style. They are intended only to help students start thinking about how they learn.

There are many ways to look at learning styles. Bernice McCarthy, in *The 4MAT System: Teaching to Learning Styles with Right/Left Mode Techniques* (Excel, Inc., 1987), identified four learning styles. Style 1 learners want to make information relevant to their lives. Style 2 learners like to observe and analyze what they learn. Style 3 learners want to improve, apply and experiment with information. Style 4 learners prefer to *use* information, and they learn best by doing.

In *The Gregoric Style Delineator* (Gabriel Systems, Inc., 1984), Anthony F. Gregoric, Ph.D., and Dr. Kathleen Butler describe four major types of learning styles. Concrete Sequentials learn best in an orderly environment, working step by step with factual information. Abstract Sequentials like to work alone and learn in a traditional manner, relying on lecture notes, experts and references. Concrete Randoms are self-directed and competitive, preferring open-ended activities and experimentation. Abstract Randoms learn best when allowed to be flexible and creative and to work with other people in an atmosphere that is competitive.

Another popular test, the *Herrmann Brain Dominance Profile*, Ned Herrmann Group (Applied Creative Services, Ltd., 1993), divides the brain into four quadrants and tests people to find out what part of the brain they use most. Someone who thinks more with the Upper Left likes facts, is very logical and works best when analyzing and problem-solving. The Lower Left dominant person is detail-oriented, organized, likes to plan and to control situations. The Lower Right person expresses a lot of emotions, senses and perceives, is people-oriented and talks a lot. The Upper Right person tends to be imaginative, artistic and unorthodox.

There are, of course, other ways to describe learning styles. You may want to give your students an actual learning styles test, if you have one available. If not, the following activities can help students start thinking about *how* they learn, instead of *what* they learn. For many young people, that will be an important first step towards understanding themselves and how they function best.

When introducing "The One and Only You" activities, consider using yourself as an example first. Show students some of *your* learning style characteristics. That will help them start to see that people have different ways of learning.

The One and Only YOU

Your Personal Learning Style

Everyone's always telling me to be myself. I don't even know who that is yet.

Angela on "My So-Called Life"

Do you have a certain style when you dress? Some students prefer to wear only black, and others like the "I work out every day" look of Spandex. Some like the wholesome look of khaki pants and polo shorts, while others like skeleton earrings and T-shirts with pictures of heavy metal bands.

Just as people have styles of dress, they also have styles of learning. However, most people haven't given nearly as much thought to their learning styles as they have to their clothing styles.

What is a learning style? It is a combination of characteristics that describes how a person learns best. Your combination will be different than your friend's combination or your brother's and sister's combination, though there may be some similarities. Your learning style is like a fingerprint. No one but you has the ridges and swirls that make a fingerprint yours. Similarly, no one but you has the unique collection of characteristics that makes up your learning style.

Perhaps you have never before thought about how you learn. Take a look at some of the characteristics listed below. In each set, mark the description that sounds most like you. If neither one fits, write your own description in the space provided.

Morning Learner

You are most energetic in the morning. You have no trouble getting up when the alarm rings. You would rather get up at 5:00 a.m. to study for a test than stay up past midnight studying.

Night Learner

You don't really get going until after lunch. You hate getting up in the morning, but you can easily stay up until the wee hours of the morning. You study much better at night than during the day.

_____ **Learner**

"Color in the Lines" Learner

You like things to be done "right." You would never color outside the lines or color a tree purple. You like it when a teacher gives very precise instructions like, "The paper is due Friday, no exceptions."

"Color Trees Purple" Learner

You think there are *lots* of "right" ways to do something. Trees can be green, but sometimes it's fun to make them purple. You like it when a teacher gives flexible instructions like, "I'd like to have your papers by Friday, but Monday's okay, too. You decide if you want to work on the weekend."

_____Learner

"Let's Be Logical" Learner

You make decisions by looking at a whole lot of factors and then weighing all the facts carefully. If you have to choose which sport to go out for, you might look at who is coaching, the hours that the team will practice, the popularity of the sport and what other school activities meet at the same time. Then you make a logical choice, for you.

"It Feels Right" Learner

You rely a lot on your intuition. You go by what feels right, without analyzing why. If you have to choose which sport to go out for, you won't have to think about it much. You will just "know" which one is right for you, based on a feeling you have.

_____Learner

Listener

You can learn a lot by listening to someone explain something. You have no trouble paying attention to lectures or lessons in class, as long as the teacher is halfway interesting.

See-er

It's very hard for you to "get" something by listening. If someone *tells* you directions for finding an address, you will probably have trouble finding it. However, if someone shows you a map you can *look* at, you will have no problem at all.

_____**Learner**

Competitor

You thrive when there's competition, either individual competition or team competition. You like to try to write the funniest skit for drama class, or get the highest score on the math test.

Cooperator

Competition just makes you nervous. You would rather write a funny skit for drama and then let others help you make it better — while you give suggestions for *their* skits. Getting the highest "A" wouldn't make you feel much better than getting an "A," period.

_____**Learner**

Watcher

You understand how to do something by watching someone do it. For example, if the auto mechanics teacher shows you how to change a tire, you will understand and remember how to do it.

Doer

You learn best by *doing*. You could never learn how to change a tire without going through the steps yourself.

_____**Learner**

"Nice and Tidy" Learner

You like to have your books neatly stacked and your desk tidy. You want your pencils sharpened and everything "just so" before you get started.

"Don't Mind the Mess" Learner

Your locker is a mess and so is your desk, if you even use a desk at all. No one could find anything in your backpack, except you. *You* know where things are, more or less, and that's okay with you.

_____**Learner**

"By Myself"
Learner

You like people, but you work best alone. You find it distracting to study with friends. (You may have more *fun,* but you know you aren't learning as much.)

"Let's Do It Together"
Learner

You work best when other people are involved somehow. When reviewing for a test, you do best if a parent or a friend asks you questions about the material. You love group projects and do well at them.

_____**Learner**

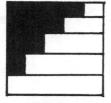

Step-by-Stepper

You like to do things in order. If you are writing a short story for a class, you will decide on the characters, outline a plot and then plan the story, step by step. *Then* you will start writing.

Zig-Zagger

You may start in the middle of something and work backwards. If you are writing a short story, you might write down a whole bunch of ideas all over the page, cross out some of them, and begin by writing the big battle scene at the end of the story.

_____**Learner**

Active Learner

You jump from one subject to the next when you study, and you fidget a lot. You are easily distracted.

Calm Learner

You easily fall asleep when studying or even when taking a test. You are very calm.

_____ **Learner**

Cautious Learner

You do only what you know the teacher wants. You make sure your answer is correct before you raise your hand. You follow the instructions for an assignment exactly.

Free Spirit

You like to try different things. You will put your own special twist on an assignment. You aren't afraid to speak up in class.

_____ **Learner**

What else do you know about how you learn and study best? Make up names for other characteristics that describe you. Then describe those characteristics.

_____

_____

_____

Name _____

The One and Only YOU
A Description of Your Learning Style

Know thyself.

— Socrates

Take all the characteristics that you marked in "The One and Only You — Your Personal Learning Style." Now write a description of all you know so far about your learning style. If you want, you might even draw a picture of your learning style, as you imagine it.

For example, here's the description a boy named Owen wrote, along with his picture:

I drew my learning style with a bunch of squiggles. That's because I don't ever do anything in a straight or neat way. I'm kind of "all over the place." I'm also an active learner and have a hard time sitting still. That's why I don't like school a whole lot, at least most of the time. I have the sun coming up over my squiggles because I'm a morning person. My mom says I've always been that way, even when I was a baby. I would wake up at 5:00 a.m. and start crying. (She didn't like that much because she's a night person.)

I'm also a "color trees purple" person. I hate having to do stuff according to the rules. I hate rules, period. I'm also a "feels right" learner. I don't like to be logical. I'm also a see-er. (That's why the eye is in my picture.) I don't listen real well. My dad says what he says to me goes in one ear and out the other.

I'm definitely a "don't-mind-the-mess" person. I like to put things in piles around my room. Nobody else can figure out the piles, but I can. I'm also a group person. My best tests have been when my big sister helped me study. I'm also a zig-zagger. I guess that goes with not liking logical stuff. I'm also a free spirit. I sure don't have any trouble speaking up in class. Some of my teachers probably wish I didn't speak up so much.

I also call myself a people person. I like stuff with people involved somehow. That's why there are people sticking out of my squiggles. Like in math, it may be weird, but I like the story problems a lot better than a page of number problems to do. I think it's because the story problems have people in them. Another thing I am is an optimistic person. I don't worry much. I always figure things will work out. I don't look at the bad stuff, just the good stuff.

The One and Only YOU

An Action Plan

Each player must accept the cards life deals him. But once they are in hand, he alone must decide how to play the cards in order to win the game.

— Voltaire

Choose three characteristics from your own personal learning style. (See "The One and Only You — Your Personal Learning Style," page 63.) How could you use knowledge about this learning style to improve how you do in school? Be sure to talk to other people, both adults and young people, for ideas.

Here's an example. Three characteristics in Owen's learning style (page 69) are "active learner," "see-er" and "color trees purple" learner. Here is his action plan:

For "active learner" — If I write down things when the teacher is talking, it will help me focus. If I just sit and try to listen, I space out everything the teacher says. I don't have to really take notes. I can just write down words the teacher says, to keep my attention on what he is saying.

I can also try to set small goals for myself, like "I'll sit here until I get 10 math problems done; then I'll set a timer and shoot baskets for five minutes. Then I'll come back and do 10 more problems."

For "see-er" — Whenever I can, I'll try to *read* instructions, instead of just listening to the teacher's. I do better with what I can see. When I listen to a lesson, I'll try to draw pictures about what the teacher is saying. If she's talking about the War of 1812, I might print "1812" in real neat letters and then draw two guys battling while she's talking.

For "color trees purple" learner — I'll try to look at ways to make an assignment more interesting to *me*. If I have to do a report on volcanoes, I'll do it, but I'll add a "just-for-fun" section at the end, like a list of movies with volcanoes in them. I'll try asking the teacher if I can change the assignment a little. (Example: How about if I write a play about that battle and videotape it, instead of doing a report? I can do the same research and get across the same information, but it will be more interesting to me.) Sometimes teachers don't mind if you have a different idea, and some even like it.

Looking ☆ at ☆ Attitudes

Looking at Attitudes

This chapter helps students look at how attitudes affect what we do, what happens to us and how people respond to us. It also helps students learn ways to *change* when an attitude or an approach is not working out.

Teacher InstructionS for

It's Not My Fault!
INTRODUCING WABS

A MILLION EXCUSES
WABs in Trouble

Are we becoming a society of WABs — **W**hiners **A**nd **B**lamers? Some people think so. Certainly our schools have their share of them. "It's not my fault!" a student will say, explaining why he slugged another boy in the hall. "But I wanted to go to the mall!" another will whine, as if that's a good reason for not doing her geography homework.

Sometimes the best way to address a serious subject is with humor. While students often have an amazing capacity for ignoring advice, speeches and lectures on a topic, poking fun at the same topic can have a big impact. After students complete "It's Not My Fault," "A Million Excuses" and "The Ultimate WAB," they will be much more aware of how ridiculous it is to blame others for problems that are their own.

It's Not My Fault!
INTRODUCING WABS

I merely took the energy it takes to pout and wrote some blues.

Duke Ellington

Everybody has met a WAB. Most of us have even *been* a WAB once in awhile. What is a WAB? This short play will tell you.

Characters:

Brad, a student
Gina, a student

Brad: I don't want to go home tonight. I'm getting an "F" in math.

Gina: You're parents are going to be pretty mad.

Brad: Yes, but they shouldn't be. It's not *my* fault.

Gina: It's not? How come?

Brad: Well, for one thing the teacher doesn't like me.

Gina: Why not?

Brad: I don't know. You know how teachers are. Besides, she's really boring. And the subject is boring too.

Gina: I don't think math is that boring. It's sure not as boring as social studies.

Brad: Well, I also lost my math book.

Gina: You can borrow mine sometimes.

Brad: It won't help. I also lost my notebook. And someone stole my pencils.

Gina: I've got an extra pencil you can have. Just a second . . .

Brad: It won't help. I hate that class. None of my friends are there.

Gina: Well, at least you don't have any distractions.

Brad: Wrong. I can't concentrate because Andrea Ward sits right in front of me, and you know how gorgeous she is.

Gina: That's true. I suppose that would make it hard to concentrate.

Brad: It wouldn't matter if I *could* concentrate. The teacher hates boys.

Gina:	Really? I never noticed that. What about her two sons? Does she beat them or anything?
Brad:	Probably. She's totally unreasonable. She even expects me to do homework on Wednesday nights, and my favorite TV shows are on Wednesday.
Gina:	Maybe you could get up real early on Thursday and do your homework.
Brad:	It wouldn't work. My stupid alarm clock doesn't work right. I'm late half the time and miss part of the lesson.
Gina:	Maybe your parents could help you catch up.
Brad:	My mother isn't good at math either, so she can't help me.
Gina:	What about your dad?
Brad	I only see him on weekends. I don't want to bother him for help then, since I don't see him very much.
Gina:	Couldn't you ask the teacher for help?
Brad:	Haven't you been listening? She hates boys.
Gina:	I forgot.
Brad:	Besides that, this girl I know in class is always passing me notes.
Gina:	And I guess she would be mad at you if you didn't answer them.
Brad:	Of course. And then Alex Wanner is in the class, and he's always getting me in trouble.
Gina:	How?
Brad:	You know . . . goofing around. Half the time I can't even hear what the assignment is.
Gina:	Does it matter? I thought you didn't do the assignments anyway.
Brad:	Well, I can't. I've got English second period, so I've got to get my English homework done during math.
Gina:	You mean when you're not goofing off with Alex or passing notes to Andrea.
Brad:	Right. Sometimes it's hard to do anything, though. I'm always so hungry I can't concentrate, since I never have breakfast.
Gina:	I know — because your alarm doesn't work right and you don't have time.
Brad:	Finally, you're listening. Like I said, it's not *my* fault I'm failing.

Brad is a WAB. WAB stands for **W**hiner **A**nd **B**lamer. A WAB's entire life is controlled by other people and outside forces. True WABs believe that nothing is ever their fault. If you ask them, "Who is responsible for your actions?" they look puzzled. "Not me, of course," they seem to be thinking.

WABs whine. WABs blame. WABs *never* look to see how their actions might have an impact on what happens to them. In short, WABs are immature and often very annoying.

Unfortunately, young WABs often grow up to be adult WABs. Let's look at one of them.

Marla is a thirty-five year old mail carrier who is not doing very well at her job. She has received a number of warnings at work, and she suspects she is about to be fired. It is not her fault, of course.

One day Marla makes the mistake of complaining about her situation to Steve, a friend of hers who is very anti-WAB. Let's look at how Steve reacts to Marla.

Characters

Marla
Steve

Marla: I don't know what I'm going to do if I lose my job, Steve. I've already had three warnings, and I'm afraid my supervisor is about to fire me.

Steve: What's the problem?

Marla: My supervisor just doesn't like me.

Steve: Really? How come?

Marla: Who knows? She's always complaining about how I don't do my share. She's *so* unreasonable.

Steve: That must be tough.

Marla: Plus, she's so BORING. How can anyone expect me to do my job around someone as boring as her?

Steve: My boss is not exactly Mr. Excitement, either, but there's not much I can do about it. But having a boring supervisor doesn't really keep me from sorting mail, to tell you the truth.

Marla: Sorting mail is boring, too.

Steve: Well, yes. But I figure that I don't have to do it forever, and all jobs have their ups and downs. Maybe if you work real hard at it you can get promoted into a job you like better.

Marla: If you're so smart, tell me how I should deal with *this* problem: I have to work with this woman I can't stand.

Steve: Doesn't everybody? I mean, at every job I've ever had there's been somebody I didn't care for much. You just have to deal with it. People are people, and they just don't always like each other.

Marla: But she's always complaining about everything.

Steve:	(Sighing) I sure can see how that could be annoying. . . So what else is wrong?
Marla:	I can't concentrate, either.
Steve:	Why not?
Marla:	I have to deliver mail to an office where this really handsome guy works. Every time I get in that office building, I just go to pieces. I can't concentrate at all.
Steve:	(Starting to become a bit sarcastic) How unreasonable! No mail carrier should have to deliver mail to buildings where good-looking people might be a distraction.
Marla:	Exactly. And what's worse is that my supervisor hates women.
Steve:	Really? Isn't she a woman herself?
Marla:	You're getting off the subject. Since she's a woman, you'd think she'd have a little more sympathy. My boyfriend is always calling me at work and getting me in trouble. I can't help it if he's the jealous type and needs to check up on me all the time. She should understand that.
Steve:	Of course. After all, *you* don't have anything to do with your choice of boyfriends.
Marla:	Now you're starting to understand. It's also not my fault that I can't remember the names of the streets where I'm supposed to deliver the mail.
Steve:	Of course not. The city should change all the names to simple ones, like "First" and "Second" and "Third" streets. Go ahead and get it all out, Marla. What else is wrong?

Continue the play. What other complaints does Marla have? How does Steve answer her?

A MILLION EXCUSES
W A B s i n T r o u b l e

He who makes excuses accuses himself.

a French proverb

Michael and Holly are both WABS in trouble with their parents. Help them out by coming up with a million excuses for why their problems are not their fault. (If you can't think of a million excuses, try for a least 25 each.)

Holly

Although she was not supposed to have anyone over, Holly invites six friends over for a party while her parents are gone for the weekend. The six friends invite several more friends, who invite eight more. Holly winds up with a house full of people, and she doesn't even know a lot of them. Things get out of control, and there is a lot of damage to the house. Eventually the neighbors call the police.

Holly says nothing is her fault. List her excuses.

Michael

Michael runs over to his friend Jody's house for "just a minute" while he is supposed to be baby-sitting his five-year-old brother Zachary. While he is gone, Zachary decides to make a peanut butter and jelly sandwich and take it to the cocker spaniel puppy in the yard at the end of the block. When Michael comes back, there is grape jelly all over the beige carpet in the living room. The front door is open, and Zachary is nowhere to be found. Just then Michael's parents arrive home.

Michael says nothing is his fault. List his excuses.

Facing the music

Now imagine that Holly and Michael are *not* WABs. Describe what they might say in dealing with the above situations if they were *not* being "WAB-ish."

Teacher Instructions for

The Ultimate W.A.B.
WHINER AND BLAMER

Role playing

Students can sometimes learn a lot by taking something to an extreme. Have them try creating the ultimate WAB — in other words, the most extreme WAB they can imagine. One effective way to do that is through role playing.

Ask for volunteers. Give each volunteer one of the situations below, and explain that the students are to pretend they are the WABs involved. One at a time, they will tell about their problem and describe why it is not their fault. Encourage them to be as outrageous as possible.

The situations:

- You are a seven-year-old who just threw a baseball through your neighbor's new window. Tell why it wasn't your fault.

- You are a football player on the team that just lost the state championship. Tell why it wasn't the team's fault.

- You are a workaholic whose wife has just left you. Explain why her leaving had *nothing* to do with you.

- You just got suspended from school for your behavior. Explain why the suspension was unfair.

- You are the president of a company, and your firm just failed to meet an important delivery deadline. Explain why the problem isn't your fault.

- You are a senior in high school, but you don't have enough credits to graduate with your class. Explain why you are not to blame.

By exaggerating the whining and blaming, students will become much more conscious of how ridiculous excuse-making can be.

More WAB activities:

After students complete "It's Not My Fault!" and "A Million Excuses," ask them to watch for examples of both WAB-ish and *non*-WAB-ish behavior in newspaper and television stories. You might even want to have a special bulletin board or display for the stories collected.

- A man on trial for murder admits killing his wife. He explains that it wasn't his fault, though, because he was drunk.

- An armed robber shoots a clerk in the back, but he says it is not his fault she is paralyzed. After all, she moved when he told her not to.

- A student's parents sue the school because their son failed chemistry. They explain that the school did not notify them that their son was not doing his homework.

Examples of non-WAB-ish, responsible behavior:

- An appliance company with a defective toaster lever recalls the toasters and replaces them free of charge.

- A senator insults someone in a speech. Later he apologizes, saying only, "I made a mistake and I'm sorry."

- A plumbing contractor admits that his employees made a mistake that led to water damage in a new building. The contractor pays for the repairs.

Teacher Instructions
for
When You're Stuck, Do Something
Different

"When You're Stuck, Do Something Different" is an activity that addresses an all-too-common problem: the human tendency to try the same thing over and over again, even if it doesn't work. (In fact, our tendency is often to try that same thing even harder!)

The story about Carmichael and Pete illustrates a problem and then shows how Pete finally deals with it by changing — not Charmichael's — but his *own* behavior.

You might want to try the activity more than once. When students are asked to list some things that happen to them again and again, have them come up with school-related items the first time through, including at least one item that they are willing to share. Then, after they have tried the change for a week, have them write about (or discuss) the results. What happened? Did the change help in any way? If so, how?

The second time through, ask students to come up with their own private list of things that happen again and again. This time they don't need to share either their list or the change they are going to try. At the end of the week, ask them to report only whether or not their change had any positive results.

The reason for the privacy? Sometimes the things that bother students the most are things that they wouldn't (and shouldn't) want to bring up in class. With a bit of encouragement, however, they may be willing to address some problems that have really been bothering them. The assignment gives them encouragement, yet also allows them privacy.

Be sure students understand that changes don't always bring good results. Sometimes people try something different, and the results are worse than they were before. Still, they may have benefited just from getting "unstuck." They can go on and try something else that *might* work.

When You're Stuck, Do Something
Different

In the middle of difficulty lies opportunity.

— Albert Einstein

Human beings are sometimes funny creatures. As intelligent as we may be, we often act in very illogical ways. For example, human beings are very resistant to change. If something isn't working out the way we would like, do we think of changing? No. Too often, we try the same thing we've always done, only harder.

Pete, for example, is always trying to get his best friend Carmichael to be on time. Whenever they are supposed to meet somewhere, Carmichael is at least a half an hour late. By the time he gets there, Pete is furious because he has had to wait so long. He yells at Carmichael, who always apologizes and gives him an excuse.

The same situation occurs again and again. Pete always yells. Carmichael always apologizes and gives Pete an excuse. Nothing changes. The next time they meet, Carmichael is late again.

One day someone pointed out this quotation to Pete:

**"If you always do what you've always done,
you always get what you've always gotten."**

— Anonymous

Pete started thinking about that. Why did he keep doing the same thing over and over again? It didn't make much sense to wait for Carmichael all the time and start out being mad at him. What if he did something different? Would he *get* something different?

He thought a lot, and he talked to some friends for ideas. What could he do differently? He and his friends came up with three ideas:

- He could always arrive half an hour late himself.
- He could leave if Carmichael wasn't there on time.
- He could bring another friend along so it wouldn't be so boring to wait for Carmichael.

Pete decided to try combining the last two ideas. He would leave if Carmichael wasn't there on time, and he would bring a friend along. That way he would still get to do the planned activity, but without Carmichael.

When they made plans to go to a movie, Pete told Carmichael that he wasn't going to wait on him if he wasn't on time. Of course, he had always told Carmichael that before, so Carmichael didn't believe him. Sure enough, Carmichael arrived late. This time Pete wasn't around. He had brought a friend along, and the two of them had gone on to the movie.

Carmichael was mad. Pete stayed calm when he saw him. "Why are you mad?" he asked. "I told you I wouldn't wait around any more." Then he changed the subject.

The next time they were to meet, Pete tried the same thing. Carmichael was late again. Pete was gone. Again Carmichael was mad. Again Pete stayed calm.

The third time they were to meet, Carmichael was on time.

Is Carmichael always on time now? No. But he is on time when he is supposed to meet Pete, at least most of the time. He knows that Pete won't be around if he isn't. Because Pete was finally willing to *do* something different, he got something different in return. At first the something different was an angry friend. But eventually he got a friend who was on time — just what he had always wanted in the first place.

Think about your life. What happens to you again and again, though you wish it wouldn't? A few examples:

- I do poorly on tests.
- My brother is always picking a fight with me.
- I get sent to the office a lot.
- I'm always missing the bus on Monday mornings.
- I do my work but forget to hand it in.

Describe what happens to you:

_____

_____

_____

_____

_____

_____

_____

Think about the quotation Pete heard: "If you always do what you've always done, you always get what you've always gotten."

Now take a close look at what you always do. Think about *one* positive thing you could try to do differently for a week. It doesn't have to be a big thing. Just keep thinking, "If what I'm doing isn't working very well, I'll do something different and see what happens. I'm going to be willing to change."

For example, a number of students in one class said, "I always do poorly on tests." Each student decided to try one change. Here are the changes they came up with:

- Kirstin decided to try studying for science tests in the morning instead of at night when she was tired.

- Randy decided to try studying, period. He had never bothered before.

- Ethan decided to read the chapter in the social studies book the night before he had a test in social studies.

- Audrey decided to go into the bathroom and do deep breathing exercises before her math tests. She always "froze up" during tests.

- Tori decided to try paying attention in English for one week, instead of writing notes and talking to her friend Cara.

Some of the changes helped, and some of them didn't. Each student then tried *another* change. All of them eventually saw some improvement in their test scores, and some of them improved a lot.

Now choose one area of school where you aren't satisfied. Decide on one change to try in the next week. What will you do differently? Be specific.

_____

_____

_____

_____

_____

At the end of a week, write down your observations. What effect or effects did your change have? What was different? Was it a good difference? Did any of the effects change over the course of the week? Explain.

_____

_____

_____

_____

_____

_____

_____

_____

_____

_____

_____

*You feel the way you do right now because of
the thoughts you are thinking at this moment.*

David D. Burns

Many people have found that pretending can help them change habits. How? Read these three short scenes to find out:

The pretenders

(Characters: Maria and Chris)

Maria: I have a tendency to be shy, so I don't get to meet or get to know many people. Sometimes if I'm going to a party, I pretend that I'm not shy. I pretend that I'm really outgoing.

Chris: How do you do that?

Maria: Well, I lie down before I go and close my eyes. Then I imagine myself smiling and talking to people and being friendly.

Chris: What happens?

Maria: It's the funniest thing — when I pretend that I am really outgoing, I really do become more outgoing. I have a lot more fun.

Chris: I know what you mean. I have never been able to draw, not even decent stick figures. Then I got stuck in a drawing class last quarter. I pretended that I could draw.

Maria: And you could?

Chris: Well, I wasn't Leonardo da Vinci. But I was a whole lot better than I ever thought I could be.

Accordion-playing business owner

(Characters: Sharon and Dave)

Sharon: I hate getting up in front of people. I really, really hate it, but I often have to do it as part of my job. A long time ago, I learned to pretend, and that really helps.

Dave: What do you mean?

Sharon:	Well, when I was a kid, I played — now don't laugh — the accordion. My parents made me enter contests and perform at meetings and programs all over the place. I hated it. I was very shy and had to stand there facing the audience. It's not like playing the piano, where you can sort of hide.
Dave:	It sounds horrible. What did you do?
Sharon:	I started pretending. I would pretend to be someone who loved what she was doing. I would smile and act like I was having a good time. People started saying, "Oh, you just look so happy up there. It was wonderful to hear you and watch you." People loved it, and when I pretended I was having fun I found that I . . .
Dave:	I can guess. You found that you really did have fun.
Sharon:	No. I still hated it, but I didn't hate it nearly as much. By pretending I felt a certain way, I really helped change how I felt. Today, when I have to give talks and presentations as part of my job, I pretend that I know what I'm doing and that I like it. Then I do just fine.

Algebra hater

(Characters:	Malcolm and Kevin)
Malcolm:	I hate algebra. I mean, I really, really, really, really hate algebra.
Kevin:	Don't hold back now. Tell us how you honestly feel.
Malcolm:	I really, really, really, really, really, really, really hate algebra.
Kevin:	Okay. So what's your point?
Malcolm:	My point is, I listened to Maria and Chris and decided to try pretending. I figured, "What do I have to lose? After all, I . . . "
Kevin:	I know — You really, really, really, really, really hate algebra.
Malcolm:	Right. So I started pretending I loved it, just to see what would happen.
Kevin:	What did you do?
Malcolm:	Well, partly I just tried to think differently. When we got a really, really, really awful assignment, I tried not to think to myself, "I really, really, really hate this." I'd say things to myself like, "This should be an interesting challenge for me tonight." I felt stupid doing it, but I did it.
Kevin:	And what happened?
Malcolm:	I'd have a hard time with the assignment, and I wouldn't like it. But I didn't really, really, really, really *hate* it. Pretending did seem to help.
Kevin:	What else did you do?

Malcolm: I just pretended the class was interesting. Maybe that helped me understand better. Or maybe the teacher liked me better because I wasn't moaning and groaning and making gagging noises all the time. Who knows? Whatever it was, I did start doing better, and I didn't hate it nearly as much.

Try pretending

Think of an area where you could do better. For one week, pretend. Pretend whatever seems appropriate for the area where you have difficulty. Here are some examples:

- Pretend that you don't mind getting up in front of people to give speeches, even though you do.

- If you really hate a teacher, pretend that he or she is not so bad for a week.

- If your little sister drives you nuts, pretend that she doesn't bother you at all.

- If you hate to read, pretend that you enjoy it.

- If you hate paying attention in Spanish class, pretend that you really want to learn the language.

- If you hate running laps, pretend that running is your favorite thing in the world. (You might even go further and imagine yourself as a championship runner.)

Choose two areas in which you will pretend for the next week. Now list specifically what you will pretend in each area. (Note: You do not need to share this list unless you want to.)

1. _____

_____

_____

2. _____

_____

_____

At the end of a week, write down your observations. Did pretending help you in any way? Be honest. If so, why do you think it helped? If it didn't help, what do you think might have gotten in the way? (If you chose not to share your list, just write *generally* about the success of your pretending. You don't need to share specifics unless you feel comfortable doing so.)

LOWER YOUR GOALS?

Artists who seek perfection in everything are those who cannot attain it in anything.
Eugene Delacroix

Have you ever heard the advice, "Aim high and fall low?" That's usually very good advice. If you set high goals and fall short of them, you have still achieved a high goal — just not as high as you set out to achieve. Sometimes, however, the "Aim high and fall low" approach is not the best, especially if you are either a perfectionist or someone who has trouble getting started with anything.

There are two problems with the "aim high" approach:

- If you always set goals that are impossible to achieve, you always feel like a failure, even if you are accomplishing a great deal.

- If you set high goals, you may find yourself thinking that it is impossible to meet them. As a result, you never even try.

There are times when it pays to ignore the traditional advice to "Aim high and fall low." There are times when it is actually more helpful to aim lower, starting with goals that you can easily achieve. The young people below actually achieved more by trying to do *less*.

Tamara, the runner

Tamara decided to start running for exercise. Her goal was to run for half an hour a day, five times a week.

However, she found that she couldn't do it. She got tired after only about ten minutes and felt terrible. She was so discouraged that soon she didn't run at all.

A friend suggested that Tamara lower her goal to something she could easily achieve. The friend suggested that Tamara walk for a half hour every day and set a goal of running for just three blocks.

Tamara tried it. Each day she ran for three blocks and felt good that she had met her goal. She felt so good that she usually went ahead and ran farther. The result? Tamara got exercise every day and learned to feel successful about meeting her goals. Then she started moving her goal up very slowly, first to four blocks, then to five blocks — but always staying at a level that was very easy to meet.

Tamara felt good about running, instead of like a failure. It turns out that she never did make it up to half an hour of running. Instead, she found that fifteen minutes of running and a half hour of walking felt just right to her.

Derek, the failing student

Derek got an "F" in four subjects first quarter. His parents were mad at him, and he was mad at himself. He knew that he never paid attention in class. He was too busy talking or writing notes to his friend Allison, or drawing race cars in his notebook. He decided that the next quarter he would pay attention all the time. He would never write notes or talk to his friends or draw race cars.

In two days, he gave up. Meeting his goal was just too hard. He wound up with five "F's" second quarter.

For the third quarter, Derek decided to aim lower, making just one small goal a week that he could easily meet. He started with his hardest class, math. He decided *not* to draw race cars in math class when he was supposed to be working on an assignment.

At the end of a week, he was successful, and he didn't feel quite as lost in math. Doing *one* thing to improve had made him feel successful. He added another goal for math: He would skip writing notes to Allison that period and talk to her at lunch instead. At the end of another week, he felt good about meeting his goal.

As he felt success, Derek started adding more goals, one at a time — always goals that he felt sure he could meet. If a goal seemed too hard, he broke it down and tried an easier chunk. For example, he thought he could never ever do math homework every single night of the week, as his teacher expected. Doing it two nights a week seemed possible, though, so he made doing homework on Tuesdays and Thursdays his goal. That turned out not to be so bad, and before long he added Wednesdays. As he started understanding things better, he soon found that he wasn't even thinking about which nights were his homework nights. He was doing his homework automatically.

At the end of third quarter, he had brought his math grade up to a "C."

A lower goal

Try the lowering-your-goal approach to one area where you need to improve in school. What is the problem? What is one easy goal you could set to help deal with the problem, if only in a small way?

_____

_____

_____

_____

_____

_____

UNSTRANGLING YOURSELF

You should always be aware that your head creates your world.

Ken Keyes, Jr.

What holds you back? Are there things you would like to try that you have never tried? Are there things you would like to do that you have never done? Do you secretly wish you had the courage to act on a favorite dream?

Voices inside our heads

What holds us back is often nothing more than a nagging voice in our heads. The voice strangles us by saying things like this:

- I could never play basketball. I'm too short.
- I'm not popular enough to run for class president. I won't even think about it.
- This is too hard.
- I'm just stupid at math.
- I can't draw.
- I'm not smart enough to get an "A" in English.
- I won't bother asking. That person is way too good-looking to go out with me.
- This is impossible.

For some reason, we listen to this voice in our heads. We let it talk us out of taking risks and trying new things. We don't even bother to stop and look at whether or not the voice knows what it is talking about.

It's time to stop letting the nagging voice get away with murder. Try talking back to it and telling it to be reasonable. To give yourself some practice, talk back to the voices in the examples above. Be logical. Tell the voice why you're not going to listen. The first two are completed for you, below.

What the voice says:	What you can say back:
I can't play basketball. I'm too short.	Who says I can't play basketball? Of course I can. I can play with my friends. Maybe I can even play on the school team if I work harder than everybody else. I know that most NBA players are over six feet tall, but I might grow. Who knows? Even if I don't, I can still have a lot of fun playing basketball.
I'm not popular enough to run for class president. I won't even think about it.	I don't know how popular I am, but I do have a lot of friends. Who knows if I have enough to win an election? Maybe a lot of people who don't know me would vote for me if I made a really good speech. If I don't try, I certainly can't do it. Maybe I'll win, and maybe I won't. What's wrong with trying?

This is too hard.	
I'm just stupid at math.	
I can't draw.	
I'm not smart enough to get an "A" in English.	
I won't bother asking. That person is way too good-looking to go out with me.	
This is impossible.	

Now try talking back to your *own* voice when it is strangling you.

What the voice says:	What you can say back:

Using Study CRUTCHES

I think I can — I think I can — I think I can — I think I can.
— *The Little Engine That Could*
(Watty Piper)

Students sometimes have a negative attitude about doing school assignments. After all, studying is not easy. It's often very hard work.

That's why it's okay to use study "crutches."

If you break your leg, you can use crutches to help you get around. In the same way, you can use study crutches to help you with school work. Study crutches are the small aids and comforts that make your job easier or more fun, in even the smallest ways. Here are a few examples:

- Rachel's crutch is Coca-Cola. She feels better about studying when she's got a Coke to sip. In a pinch, a glass of iced tea or even ice water helps.
- Paul's crutch is writing with nothing but Bic pens, black only.
- Keesha's crutch is yellow legal pads. She takes notes on them and writes rough drafts of all her papers on them. She even does her math homework on them.
- Christina's crutch is having her room arranged just right before she starts studying. She pulls all the curtains, turns on her answering machine, piles her books on the night stand beside her bed, puts a big "wedge" pillow on the bed for a backrest, and turns on her lamp.
- Michael's crutch is push-ups. He does ten of them before he starts to work, and he does ten of them every half an hour while he studies.

A study crutch is something that pampers you and makes it easier to study, if only in a small way. It is *not* something that is really enjoyable but just distracts you. For example, having six friends over to talk while you write your history paper might be fun, but it is not a study crutch. It is unlikely that you would get your history paper done with six friends around.

What has helped you in the past? What do you think might help now? Experiment with some reasonable study crutches. Pamper yourself by indulging in whatever helps make studying more pleasant — and productive.

Some study crutches I know work for me:_____

_____

Some study crutches I am going to try:_____

_____

Teacher InstructionS
for

Neatness Counts

College education courses talk a lot about things like creativity, critical thinking skills, self-esteem and cognitive development. They don't mention a boring little problem that real teachers face every day: neatness — or, rather, the lack thereof.

Students often hand in papers that are scrawled in pencil on formerly wadded-up, torn sheets of paper that may even have gone through the rinse cycle while in the back pocket of a pair of jeans. They scribble out work that is unreadable and shows little or no care in preparation.

Real teachers are doing young people a disservice if they don't address the subject of appearance. Like it or not, in the real world of work, appearance matters. Sloppy memos may not be taken seriously. A presentation full of hastily-prepared visual aids may lose a client who doubts that the company is careful enough to do a good job. Auto mechanics who leave grease all over the car seats may not have a lot of repeat business. Appearance conveys an attitude.

For a visual lesson in the importance of appearance, try the following exercise:

Bake a batch of sugar cookies, or buy some from a bakery. (Two or three dozen works well.)

Next, divide the cookies into three equal groups. Frost one group of cookies, using a brightly-colored icing, or even several colors. You might even want to make ornate designs with the frosting. The important thing is that the cookies look yummy. Then arrange them attractively on a bright plate, cover them neatly with plastic wrap, and add some ribbon or a bow.

With the next group of cookies, leave off the icing — or create a grayish-colored frosting and glob it on sloppily. Place these cookies on a plain paper plate and cover them with plastic wrap.

With the third group, crush a couple of cookies. Break up others into pieces. Take a bite out of one. Dump the whole thing into a plastic bag, preferably an old one with some dried catsup on the outside.

Tell the class that you have extra cookies to give away. (Perhaps you baked too many, or you won them in a raffle and are going to share. Come up with a reason that fits you.) Show the three groups of cookies to the class, and announce that you are going to draw three names out of a hat. The people whose names are chosen will each receive one of the packages of cookies. Before you draw, give the groups of cookies different labels and ask all the students to write down which group they would most like to receive if their name is drawn.

Draw the first name and ask what group the person chose. Chances are excellent that he or she will have chosen the frosted cookies. If not, ask for a show of hands. How many picked which group? As a class, most students will have chosen the most attractive group. (Making the subject an edible one helps keep them honest. They don't want to risk losing an edible treat by being "cute" and picking the opposite of what anyone would expect.) Give the chosen plate of cookies to the person whose name you have drawn.

Draw the second and third names, and give the students their second and third choices. The second choice will probably be the grayish cookies, and the last choice will probably be the bag of crushed cookies.

Now point out that each package was made up of exactly the same number of cookies, made from exactly the same recipe. What made one group more desirable than the other was the appearance, including the packaging and the care of preparation.

Topics for discussion:

Discuss the topic of "appearance" with your students. A few questions you might ask:

- If the three groups of cookies were English papers, which one would get the best grade? Why?
- What makes you think that the attractive package contains something better than the sloppy package?
- How do appearances affect our thinking in other areas of life? (Examples: People we meet, books we read, food we select, clothing we buy, etc.)
- Are teachers affected by appearances? Could the appearance of an assignment influence them to think that it might be better or worse than it is?

You may want to explain to students that, to a teacher, assignments are like plates of cookies. Some look ordinary. Some look terrible, and you dread looking at them. Others look like someone took a lot of care with them, and you can't help but look at those papers with a very positive attitude.

Challenge students to make their next assignment like the first plate of cookies — attractive and neat with a bit of icing.

Follow-up

Follow up your cookie demonstration with the "Neatness Counts" activity on page 98. Quite often, students haven't ever paid much attention to what makes a paper look neat and attractive. They know it shouldn't have globs of crossed out scribbles, and they probably know, at least in theory, that it should have their name at the top. Beyond that, they may not have a clue. This activity helps students tune in to what makes a student's work *look* good.

Twenty-five DOs and DON'Ts is a lot, and students will have to think hard. Allow them to work in groups and consult one another for ideas. Here are some possible answers:

1. **Do** put your first and last name at the top of the page.
2. **Don't** leave spiral notebook shreds hanging raggedly from the edge where you ripped the page from your notebook.
3. **Do** type the paper, when possible.
4. **Do** write it in ink or dark, readable pencil.
5. **Do** include a heading, if your teacher wants one.
6. **Don't** leave holes where you have erased seven or eight times.
7. **Do** put a nice cover on reports and projects.
8. **Do** indent each new paragraph.
9. **Do** leave a margin at the top, bottom, left and right.
10. **Don't** write in teeny tiny handwriting that is hard to read without a magnifying glass.
11. **Don't** scribble words out. If you're writing in ink and can't erase, put one neat line through the word and then write the word correctly.
12. **Don't** write clear to the edge of the paper and then continue the sentence up the side.
13. **Do** put a title on reports and compositions.
14. **Do** capitalize the first, last and every important word of the title.
15. **Don't** write in lavender ink on lavender paper.
16. **Do** draw a picture or illustration whenever it is appropriate or you just want to make the paper look better.
17. **Do** make sure your typewriter or printer has a decent ribbon or cartridge, so that the printing is nice and clear.
18. **Don't** fold your report up and stick it in your pocket.
19. **Don't** hand in a paper with your doodles all over it.
20. **Don't** set a soda glass or coffee cup on your homework.
21. **Don't** use two different colored pens or paper for the same assignment.
22. **Don't** write on weird-sized paper.
23. **Do** write clearly. Make sure your "i's" don't look like "l's" and your "g's" don't look like "q's."
24. **Do** cross all your "t's" and dot all your "i's."
25. **Don't** dot your "i's" with circles, stars or hearts.

Neatness Counts

Did you wash your hands yet?

Everybody's mother

Imagine that you have won a million dollars in a drawing sponsored by a retired teacher who has inherited billions. There's only one catch — to collect it, you have to turn in all of the assignments you have due this week, and all of them have to *look* like "A" papers.

Yes, they only have to *look* like "A" papers. If you happen to miss 14 math problems and misspell 23 words on a report, you will still get your money, as long as the papers *look* good. (Of course, it will be better if you get all the math problems right and spell all the words perfectly. However, for the million dollars, the only thing that matters is *looks*.)

Now why would a teacher do such a thing? This particular teacher spent thirty years grading papers, and he never stopped being amazed by how little attention students pay to appearance. He thought he would go blind trying to read sloppy handwriting and smeared ink. He was sickened by crinkled-up papers, scrawled on the wrong side of the page with one corner torn off.

He could never understand why students didn't look over their work before they handed it in, why they didn't care what their papers said about them, why they didn't understand that appearance *does* count, whether we like it or not. By giving away a million dollars every year for neat papers, he hopes to make students at least pay attention to what makes an "A" paper look like an "A" paper.

You know you want the million dollars. You know you need to be careful. Come up with a checklist of 25 DOs and DON'Ts for creating a paper that gets an *A* for looks.

Example

1. **Do** put your first and last name at the top of the page.
2. **Don't** leave spiral notebook shreds hanging raggedly from the edge where you ripped the page from your notebook.

(Continue — neatly, of course — on your own paper.)

Don't put off for tomorrow what you can do today,
because if you enjoy it today, you can do it again tomorrow.

James A. Michener

What is procrastination? It is putting things off. You are procrastinating if you have ever used excuses similar to these:

- Maybe if I wait to do this history paper until later, it will be easier.

- I'll just watch one more rerun of *Star Trek*; then I'll do my homework.

- As soon as my sister gets off the phone, I'll make calls. Then I'll start my math.

- If I can get to this last level on my new video game, then I'll be in a much better mood to start my research paper.

Nearly everyone has procrastinated at some time, and it's easy to think that procrastination is "no big deal." And it probably isn't, if it only happens now and then. If it becomes a habit, however, it *can* be a problem.

Why? Because chronic procrastinators cause many problems for both themselves and others. As a procrastinator gets older, the consequences can be a lot greater than a low grade. Imagine the following excuses from an adult:

- As soon as I finish reading this new novel, I'll get up and make dinner. The kids won't mind waiting a couple of extra hours to eat.

- This hot bath feels so good; I think I'll just stay here for another half an hour. I'm sure my boss won't mind if I'm a little late for the meeting with those clients tonight.

- These letters can wait to be delivered. I just don't feel like making my rounds today.

- Those payroll checks I need to write can wait until Monday. I'd rather go play racquetball.

Everybody's got an excuse

Brainstorm a list of excuses you have used for procrastinating. (Remember: Procrastinating means to put something off until a later date.) Add excuses you have heard other people use. Here are just a few that probably sound familiar:

- I just didn't have time.

- I was too tired.

- I didn't feel like it.

- There was something I wanted to watch on television.

- _____

- _____

- _____

- _____

- _____

- _____

- _____

Ridiculous levels

Now apply at least five of the excuses on your list to a situation an adult might face. Have some fun with this. It's okay to imagine procrastination taken to ridiculous levels. Here are a few examples:

- I know that I should have paid my taxes, but I just didn't have time. I don't see why you're arresting me.

- I just don't feel like chasing that thief right now. I'm sure the chief won't mind if I try to track him down later.

- I know that house is on fire, but I'd really like to finish watching *Oprah*. Besides, the fire truck needs gas and I didn't feel like putting any in on the way back from the warehouse fire last night.

- The new president of Iran is on the phone? He sounds upset? Tell him I'd like to finish reading the paper first. I'll call him later.

- My patient's leg is broken, but I'm just not in the mood to set it right now. She can wait until I finish my golf game.

- _____

- _____

- _____

- _____

- _____

If your approach to school, work or life in general includes a lot of procrastination, you will be doing yourself a favor to change your attitude to one that more often says, "I'll do it now."

Dealing with Teachers

♣ ♦ ♥ ♠

Teachers have feelings, too.

— Mrs. Shouse, sixth grade teacher

Perfectly reasonable people sometimes act in perfectly unreasonable ways. Look at Vanessa, for example. Every day she causes problems in Mr. Nagushi's math class. She talks to her friend Kate all the time. She passes notes. She makes remarks like, "This is so boring!" when Mr. Nagushi is explaining something.

When Vanessa discovered she was going to fail the class because she hadn't turned in her homework, she went to Mr. Nagushi and asked, "Can I have some extra credit assignments?"

Mr. Nagushi said, "No."

Vanessa was furious. "He's so unreasonable!" She told everyone that Mr. Nagushi was the reason she was failing math.

Now some people might consider Vanessa the unreasonable one. She had caused Mr. Nagushi problems all quarter long. She hadn't done her work. Then when she wanted a favor, she was surprised when he didn't do what she asked. Vanessa forgot a couple of things.

- Mr. Nagushi is human. He is unlikely to feel generous toward someone who has been rude to him for weeks.
- Vanessa is responsible for her actions, not Mr. Nagushi.

Being reasonable

Students often don't realize that teachers usually respond well to any reasonable approach that students take when they have a problem. However, when students act childish, spoiled, selfish, loud, obnoxious or rude, the teachers usually aren't very sympathetic. No one, including teachers, likes to deal with someone who is acting childish, spoiled, selfish, loud, obnoxious or rude.

On the left, below, are student responses that are immature. They are *not* likely to help in dealing with teachers. On the right are some responses that teachers are much more likely to take seriously.

Immature responses

- How come you gave me a "D"?

- That's not fair.

- This is so boring.

More productive responses

- How could I do better next time?

- May I talk to you after class about this?

- (Keeping your opinion to yourself!)

Immature responses (cont.)

- You always pick on me.

- I HATE this.

- You're wrong.

- I don't get this.

So what if I made a mistake?

More productive responses (cont.)

- I made a mistake. I'll be more careful next time.

- This sure isn't my favorite thing, but I'll do my best.

- I disagree with you. Here's why:

- I'm really struggling with this. Could I get some extra help?

- I'm sorry.

Role playing or writing

Each of the scenes below involves an immature response from at least one student. With other students in your class, read aloud each of the situations, as written.

Then write or role play a different version of each scene. This time include more productive responses from the students involved. (In your version, you may even include different responses that the teacher could make. After all, teachers can often improve, too — just like any other human being.)

Scene one

Teacher: (To the class) I'm handing back all your reports on China. You'll find your grade on the back page.

Jim: (Looking on the back page) What! I can't believe you gave me a "C-" on this. I worked for three days at the library.

Teacher: (Still talking to the class) If you have any questions, I'll be happy to go over them with you. Be sure you take a look at the comments I wrote under the grade.

Jim: A "C-"! My mom is going to have a fit. I don't deserve a "C-." I wanted an "A," and I should have an "A."

Teacher: Jim, if you have a problem, talk to me after class.

Jim: My mom is going to be talking to you on the phone.

Teacher: Fine. I'll be happy to talk to her. Now, does any one else have any questions?

Jim: I hate this class.

Scene two

Teacher:	(After reading aloud a newspaper report on the increase in crime) Most of the increase in crime is obviously because of teenagers and their lack of respect for other human beings.
Karen:	Well, that's a stupid thing to say.
Teacher:	And why is it stupid?
Karen:	You just hate teenagers.
Teacher:	I think teenagers should respect other human beings, just like everyone else should.
Karen:	Well, teenagers aren't to blame for crime.
Teacher:	Who is?
Karen:	I can't believe how unfair you are. You're just prejudiced against teenagers.

Scene three

Bill:	Can I get out of class to go work on the student council posters?
Teacher:	Of course not. You've got class.
Bill:	But we never do anything anyway.
Teacher:	Sit down.
Bill:	You are so unfair. Those posters need to be done.
Teacher:	And so does your math.

Scene four

Teacher:	It's time to hand in your lab reports.
Kelly:	What! I didn't know they were due today.
Teacher:	I announced it last Friday, and it is on the board.
Kelly:	But I couldn't do it last night. I had basketball practice. Can I hand it in tomorrow?
Teacher:	Yes, but for only half credit. I told you it was due today.
Kelly:	But I need this grade.
Teacher:	I guess you should have thought of that before.
Kelly:	You're always picking on me.

ATTEMPTING THE RIMPOSSIBLE

He started to sing as he tackled the thing
That couldn't be done, and he did it.

Edgar A. Guest, *It Couldn't Be Done*

What have you always wanted to do and never had the courage to try? What would you like to try, if only you were braver or smarter or stronger or better looking or more talented? Brainstorm a list of ten things you would like to do if only you were somehow different. This can be a private list. You don't need to show it to anyone.

Here are some examples from two students' lists:

- run for student council
- try out for first chair trumpet in band
- be friends with a new girl in my class
- be on the track team
- try out for cheerleader
- learn to play chess
- try out for the school play

Some people believe that we can only accomplish what we can imagine. If we can't imagine it, we can't do it.

Pretend you have already done it

Choose one of the items from your list. Pretend that you have actually done it and have been successful. Don't write about how it would feel if you *were* to do it. Instead write as if you already *have* done it. Here's how one student began:

> *I'm really proud of myself for asking my uncle to teach me to play chess. It looked so hard, and I was afraid he'd think I was stupid. I went up to him and told him I was serious about learning, and he would be the best person to teach me . . .*

Here's how another began:

> *I'm so glad I got the courage to try out for cheerleader. It wasn't easy, but I did it! I practiced for over two hours every night, and my older sister's friends gave me a lot of pointers. I was so nervous when I got up on stage for the tryout. But I just kept thinking to myself, "You can do it!" . . . . .*

Start imagining what *you* would like to do. Your imagination may help make it a reality. It can also create a positive frame of mind that makes something *else* positive become a reality. You never know where positive thinking may lead you!

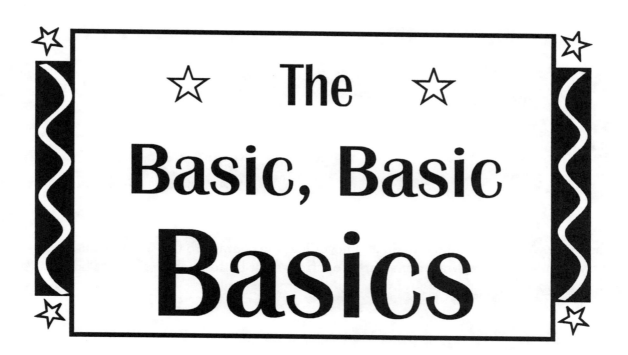

The
Basic, Basic
Basics

The Basic, Basic Basics

This final chapter is a quick look at the basics of school success. It is not intended to be comprehensive or detailed. Many books offer instructions in specifics like how to take notes, how to study for tests, how to write a research paper, etc.

This chapter is a general overview. The three activities cover the basic, basic basics of school success.

HOW TO FLUNK

A person who aims at nothing is sure to hit it.

Anonymous

Everyone always gives advice about how to do well in school. Maybe you are weird, though. Maybe you are one of those people who always does the *opposite* of what you are supposed to do. If your mother tells you to load the glasses carefully on the top shelf of the dishwasher, you put them right-side-up on the bottom shelf. If your dad tells you never ever to put your red underwear in the wash with his white shirts, you decide to see what will happen if you do. If a teacher says to put your first and last name in the upper right-hand corner of the paper, you put just your first name on the back.

If you happen to be a stubborn individualist, teachers are wise to give you different directions, like the ones below. Here are sure-fire directions for "How to Flunk Any Class":

1. Always arrive late.

2. Never slip into your desk quietly. Instead, make a big production of slamming the door behind you, shouting out, "Sorry I'm late! I had to go to the john!" If at all possible, drop all your books on the floor, too.

3. Better yet, don't have your books with you.

4. Never bring a pencil to class. Always borrow someone else's and forget to give it back.

5. Never bring paper. Let other people spend their money on stuff like that. Use their paper.

6. Use the paper you borrow to write a note. After you finish, make a big deal about passing — or better yet, *throwing* — it across the room to someone. Disturb as many people as possible.

7. Never, ever do your homework. The teacher will admire you for your consistency.

8. Lose your textbook the first week of school. Then you will have a good excuse for not reading your assignments.

9. During class, doodle on your blue jeans with a pen.

10. Draw as much attention to yourself as possible. Make funny remarks. Be loud. Start arguments.

11. Groan a lot.

12. Say, "This is BORING!" loudly every five minutes or so, especially if it is really quiet in the room.

13. Ask, "Why do we have to do this stuff?" as often as possible.

14. After the teacher says, "Turn to page 36," say, "What page?"

15. When your group or partner is depending on you, show up unprepared. Better yet, don't show up at all.

16. Turn in all of your assignments late. Better yet, never turn them in at all.

17. If you absolutely can't talk to your neighbor, stare out the window or draw airplanes on top of the desk.

18. When you get your test back with an "F," shout, "This isn't fair! The teacher hates me!"

19. Never show concern about your grade until the last day of the grading period. Then see if the teacher has extra credit you can do to make up for all 42 missing assignments.

20. If the teacher says, "no," throw a fit.

21. Torment the girl who sits in front of you. Bang your knees against the back of her chair. Show her how you can make obnoxious noises with your hand in your armpit.

22. Torment the boy who sits behind you. Steal his pencil. Jiggle his desk when he is trying to write.

23. Stay up as late as possible. Sleep in class.

24. If you have to read something in class, make it a magazine or a comic book.

25. Always chew gum, loudly.

26. If you have to do a report, copy word-for-word from the *World Book Encyclopedia*.

27. If you decide to hand in some homework, make sure you have copied it from someone else in class.

28. If you decide to do some homework for fifth period English, be sure that you do it during fourth period math.

29. Don't take notes. If you have followed items #4 and #5, this should not be a problem.

What suggestions can you add to "How to Flunk"? Write them in the space below.

_____

_____

_____

_____

_____

_____

_____

HOW TO PASS

Do what you can, with what you have, where you are.

Theodore Roosevelt

There's no secret to doing well in school. Here's how to pass just about any class in the world:

1. Show up.
2. Pay attention.
3. Do your work.
4. Behave.

Look at yourself. How well do *you* follow these four rules?

_____
_____
_____
_____
_____
_____
_____
_____
_____
_____
_____

What would you add to the list of rules? Why?

_____
_____
_____
_____

Quick Tips for Success in School

from Real People Who Have Actually Been Successful in School

Genius is one percent inspiration, ninety-nine percent perspiration.

Thomas Alva Edison

DO:

- Bring a pencil to class.
- Use your pencil for writing, not throwing.
- Put your first and last name on your paper. Don't act like you are the *only* "Clarissa" or "Zebediah" in the universe.
- Bring a notebook to class.
- Put paper in it first.
- Ask questions.
- Eat something for breakfast. A candy bar and a Coke don't count.
- Hang out with winners.
- Read.
- Read a lot.
- Break big projects into smaller chunks. Then do one chunk at a time.
- Give teachers a break sometimes if you want them to give you a break sometimes.
- Write things down so you won't forget.
- Listen when the teacher is talking. If she is really, really boring, at least be polite. Polite does not include snickering and throwing things.
- Get to know the library.
- Celebrate a job well done. Pat yourself on the back. Treat yourself to a hamburger. Tell your parents so they can brag to your grandparents.
- Learn to type.
- Follow what your "gut" tells you is right.
- Ask for help when you need it.
- Get some exercise every day. It will help you think better.

DON'T:

- Don't be an attention hog. Attention hogs get most of the attention by being a pain in the neck.
- Don't expect everything to be easy or fun.
- Don't wear headphones during class.
- Don't hang out with people you're not proud to call your friends.
- Don't ask for extra credit the day before the end of the semester, to make up for 42 missing assignments.
- Don't blame everyone else for your problems.
- Don't be afraid to be different.
- Don't say, "Somebody ripped me off!" every single time you find anything missing, from your research paper to your retainer. Look around first.
- Don't lose your math book. Or your science notes. Or your history report.
- Don't use X-rated language in class.
- Don't forget to put your name on your tests.
- Don't be mean just because someone else is.
- Don't make funny noises under your armpit during class.
- Don't yell, "I hate this stuff!" Hate it quietly, to yourself.
- Don't leave answers blank on a test. At least give them your best guess.
- Don't get a job that takes more time than your homework.
- Don't make getting a car the focus of your life.
- Don't try too hard to be funny.

DO:

- Use spare moments at school all day to do your assignments, so you don't have much homework.
- Learn to use "spell check" on a computer.
- Learn to use a computer.
- Believe that you are smart enough to figure out anything.
- Think back through your day before you go home from school. What do you need to remember?
- Do what is most important first.
- Treat others as you would like to be treated yourself. That includes teachers.
- Take three deep, slow breaths before doing anything you're nervous about.
- Sit in front, if you have a choice.
- Try out for something. Get involved.
- Discuss a complaint with a teacher privately, not in front of the whole class.
- Apologize when you know you should.
- Face the music if you get caught at something; remember all the times you *didn't* get caught.
- Remember that teachers are people, too.
- Smile at others.
- Do your best.
- Take pride in what you do.
- Copy your assignment over if it gets washed because you left it in the pocket of your jeans.
- Plan time for things that can go wrong.
- Participate in class. You'll get more out of it.
- Do your own work. Make your mistakes your own mistakes and your successes your own successes.
- Do what's right.

DON'T:

- Don't tell your math teacher you couldn't do your assignment because you had an English test.
- Don't tell your English teacher you couldn't do your assignment because you had a math test.
- Don't put off studying until you are too tired to open a book.
- Don't get peanut butter and jelly all over your homework.
- Don't write notes to your friends in class. Write them at home and pass them out between classes or at lunch.
- Don't think that you are the center of the universe and the whole school should schedule things according to your needs.
- Don't bother everyone else if you finish early.
- Don't act like a little kid if you want to be treated like a grown-up.
- Don't tattle. This is tattling: "Mr. Anderson, John just made a face at you while you weren't looking." This is *not* tattling: "Hello, 911? Someone just put a bomb in the cafeteria. Please hurry!"
- Don't write on your desk, your locker, your jeans or the bathroom walls.
- Don't have your grandmother die seven times every semester, right before tests.
- Don't sit with your best friends if they talk too much.
- Don't talk on the phone when you are reading a chapter in your science book.
- Don't think hard stuff will get easier if you put it off. It won't.
- Don't stay up late watching TV so that you can't stay awake in class.
- Don't whine.

What DOs and DON'Ts can you add to the list? Use your own ideas and also talk to others for suggestions — especially people who have done well in school.

More materials from Cottonwood Press

DownWRITE Funny
Using students' love of the ridiculous to build serious writing skills
DWFB $18.95

AbraVocabra
The amazingly sensible approach to teaching vocabulary
ABRAB...$21.95

Survival Tips for New Teachers
From people who have been there and lived to tell about it
TIPSB $7.95

Hot Fudge Monday
Tasty ways to teach parts of speech to students who have a hard time swallowing anything to do with grammar
HOTB $18.95

A Month of Fundays
A whole year of games and activities for just about every holiday you've ever heard of — and many that you haven't
FUNB $23.95

Short and Sweet
Quick creative writing activities that encourage imagination, humor and enthusiasm for writing
SSB $10.95

Journal Jumpstarts
Quick topics and tips for journal writing
JJB $7.95

Beyond Roses Are Red, Violets Are Blue
A practical guide for helping students write free verse
ROSEB...$19.95

Homework's Not Another Word for Something Else to Lose
Helping students WANT to succeed in school and then setting them up for success
HWB $19.95

Games for English and Language Arts
Reproducible games that challenge students
GEB $18.95

Ideas that Really Work!
Activities for English and Language Arts
IDB $21.95

Writing Your Lfie
Autobiographical writing activities for young people
WLTB $14.95

Surviving Last Period on Fridays and Other Desperate Situations
The Cottonwood Game Book for Language Arts
GB $14.95

When They Think They Have Nothing to Write About
The Cottonwood Composition Book
CB $14.95

Did You Really Fall into a Vat of Anchovies?
Games and activities for English and language arts
VATB $18.95

Row, Row, Row Your Class
Using music as a springboard for writing, exploration and learning
ROWB $12.95

ImaginACTION
Using drama in the classroom, no matter what you teach
IMB $14.95

Mystery of the Suffocated Seventh Grader
A play to read aloud in class
MYSB $9.95

The Case of the Colorful Kidnapping
A read-aloud play about brothers, sisters and bullies
KB $10.95

Dismissed!
A cartoon notebook for teachers
DISB $7.95

Hide Your Ex-Lax Under the Wheaties
Poems about schools, teachers, kids and education
XB $7.95

If They're Laughing, They're Not Killing Each Other
Ideas for using humor effectively in the classroom — even if you're not funny yourself
IFB $12.95

Flunk/Pass Poster Set
Two humorous, yet practical posters
POSB $6.95

and more!

Use next page to order or call for a free catalog!
1-800-864-4297

Cottonwood Press Order Blank

Quantity	Item#	Item Name	Price Each	TOTAL PRICE

Shipping and Handling	Amount ordered	Add		
	up to $16.00	$2.50	**Amount Ordered**	
	$16.01-$25.00	$3.50	Colorado residents add 3% sales tax.	
Orders are shipped UPS. Allow	$25.01-$35.00	$4.50		
3–7 business days for delivery.	$35.01-$50.00	$6.00	Shipping and Handling	
For faster delivery, call for prices.	$50.01-$75.00	$8.00		
	$75.01-$100.00	$9.00	**TOTAL**	
	$100.01 and over	add 10%		

Ship to:

Name _____

School _____
(Include only if using school address.)

Address _____
(Because we ship UPS, do not use a PO box for your address.)

City _____ State _____ Zip code _____

Daytime phone number _____
(In case we need to contact you about your order)

This is my

❑ home address   ❑ school address

Method of Payment:

❑ Check or money order *(Make payable to Cottonwood Press.)*

❑ Purchase order *(Please attach.)*

❑ VISA   ❑ MasterCard

Credit card # _____

Signature _____ Exp. date _____

PHONE:
   1-800-864-4297

MAIL:
   Cottonwood Press, Inc.
   305 West Magnolia,
   Suite 398
   Fort Collins, CO 80521

FAX:
   970-204-0761

ONLINE:
   www.verinet.com/
   cottonwood